Newsthinking

The Secret of Great Newswriting

Newsthinking the Secret of Great Newswriting

Bob Baker

Cincinnati, Ohio

Library of Congress Cataloging in Publication Data
Baker, Bob, 1947-
    Newsthinking: the secret of great newswriting.

    Bibliography: p. 195
    Includes index.
    1. Journalism—Authorship—Psychological
    aspects.
I. Title.
PN4781.B26   808'.06607021   80-27833
ISBN 0-89879-043-3

Book design by Barron Krody.
Diagrams by Donald N. Clement.

Acknowledgments

For their advice, encouragement and inspiration, thanks to Lillian and Earl Baker, Russ Barnard, Nigel Calder, Carol Cartaino, Mary Curtius, Marilyn Ferguson, Eugene Friedman, Kathy Hale, Dale Hanson, Barbara Hutmacher, William Gallagher, David Goodman, Roderic Gorney, Bob Nafius, Barbara O'Brien, Mark Shipper, Marvin Sosna, Bruce Springsteen, Ron Soderquist, A. T. Welford and Irving Werksman.

To Marjorie Baker

Contents

12.

Foreword

Good news on the newswriting front!

Here is a newswriting book that will appeal to journalism educators, students and practicing journalists alike. I had about despaired of ever seeing a fresh approach to newswriting, but now there is *Newsthinking* by Bob Baker. No mere repetition under a different cover as are so many books, *Newsthinking* points the way to a more sophisticated treatment of news reporting.

Through a creative synthesis of practice and theory, Baker has given new life to the well-worn and mundane topic of newswriting.

With innovative suggestions and concepts, helpful diagrams and fascinating insights—mainly from the field of psychology—*Newsthinking* leads the reader into a "new" world of news reporting. It shifts the emphasis of reporting from the actual act of writing to the prewriting phase—the process of thinking. This orientation is long overdue.

Most books on newswriting make their treks over familiar terrain—a little on technique, something on form and style, a bit of this and that relating to sources, interviewing and the like, something on copy preparation, some trite notes on the "inverted pyramid" story form, and the usual warnings against long words, sentences and paragraphs. Nothing really new. Nothing fresh and satisfying for the reader who desires new insights and help.

Newsthinking is certainly not such a text.

Baker maintains that newspapers, by and large, settle for very little when it comes to newswriting. He sees flaws, gaps, poor research and observation, poor interviewing, poor listening and notetaking and poor writing. I could not agree more. Newspapers in this country are big and prosperous and offer their readers highly diversified and entertaining packages for little money. But they are generally woefully shallow in newswriting.

One realizes that there is something missing in the newswriter's bag of techniques and perspectives—something that would precondition him to write a better story. And that something is a psychological sophistication that would enable him to break through the surface of news reporting and plumb the deeper meaning of a story and the motivations of the actors. From the pages that follow, the reader will be able to obtain such a sophistication if he wishes.

The "magic" which the author writes about—the psychological dimension of reporting—is much needed in today's journalism. And it will be needed increasingly in the hard, lean journalistic days ahead when technology threatens to make robopaths of us all. We need more than ever to understand ourselves, how we think, and how this thinking affects our writing.

In *Newsthinking,* the reader will find the basics of good reporting given with flair and clarity. But he will find much more: a splendid mixture of art and science, permeated with refreshing psychological and philosophical insights that add the real character to the book.

The style is direct and unpretentious; Baker has eschewed academic jargon and has pounced upon ideas with the directness and precision of a seasoned reporter and analyst.

He breathes zest into every page and takes the reader

on an intriguing tour through the world of the newswriter. The spirit of the book—an exhilarating and existential spirit—is captured early in his Rule Number 1: "There Are No Rules." I agree wholeheartedly with him when he says, "News operations that disregard this rule take on the collective mentality of the golfing gorilla"—a non-creative and robopathic mentality.

Some readers may object to the free-swinging treatment given newswriting by Bob Baker. They may yearn for yet another book which will further bind the aspiring writer in the safe and restraining harness of traditional journalistic thought and action. I hope there are not many such readers.

We have had, and have, enough "harnessed" writing and thinking. We need to dip our journalistic pens into a new ink. Journalists today—and journalism students— need to go beyond the realization that the world is complex and the news is complex; they need to get to the business of understanding that they themselves are complex, and that they cannot really divorce themselves from the news stories they write.

"I have written a news story and it is I." That is the message of a new newswriting orientation, and it is the message of this book.

It is now time to begin this exciting, eventful and profitable voyage through journalistic territory that you had perhaps thought was well-known. But now you will see it with new eyes! Bon voyage!

John C. Merrill
Director, School of Journalism
Louisiana State University
Baton Rouge

John C. Merrill, Ph.D., was a professor of journalism at the University of Missouri for fifteen years.

He has authored, coauthored or edited a dozen books on mass communication and journalism.

The most powerful drive in the ascent of man is his pleasure in his own skill. He loves to do what he does well and, having done it well, he loves to do it better.
—Jacob Bronowski

. . . be warned of the good advice of others. Be warned when they tell you that your attitude is immature. Be warned against all "good" advice because "good" advice is necessarily "safe" advice, and though it will undoubtedly follow a sane pattern, it will very likely lead one into total sterility—one of the crushing problems of our time.
—Jules Feiffer

Preface

I HATED IT.

A reporter would break his neck for hours or days, come up with first-class information and then write a second-class story. A piece that missed the point or was far too wordy or just didn't live up to its potential. He or she would romp into the city room, gleefully bellowing the juicy details, sit down at the typewriter, and an hour or two later I'd be reading the copy, shaking my head and asking myself, "What was all the fuss about?"

Of all the frustrations I encountered as a city editor, that kind of disappointment was the worst.

"You didn't *think!*" I'd complain. But the reporter could just as easily have shot back, "What the hell do you *mean,* exactly?"

I hope this book is the answer. I hope it teaches you how to think when you write a news story.

This book is devoted to improving the prewriting process—the thought process all reporters go through before they hit the first typewriter key. It is an intense examination of those moments in which you make your facts fall into place. This is *newsthinking,* where the genius of great writers—their creativity, their imagination, their willingness to take risks—unfolds. Much of it is subconscious, but most of it is also structured. The reporter or book author or magazine essayist you admire may appear to be an artist who launches his impulses from a deep, mysterious font, but in fact he is producing his mastery in a laboratory. With the sophistication of a scientist, he has built and refined a complex set of thought strategies, a system in which nothing is left to chance, where each sentence and paragraph is automatically and rigorously tested.

He knows that writing is not merely an aesthetic ballet in which words dance onto paper. Writing is thinking.

All good writers understand this, but they also know that the process is an intensely personal one built on layer after layer of habits so deeply ingrained and complex that they defy simple description. How can any writer tell you, in five or ten minutes, how he thinks a story through? As a result, many reporters—especially the successful ones—adopt the pose of artist rather than mechanic, and it's hard to blame them. After all, we merely admire proficient mechanics; we *marvel* at artists.

The goal of this book is to cut through that facade by revealing to you the thought processes and mental attitudes a highly skilled reporter uses to sort though thousands of facts and organize them into literate, perceptive and creative copy. Whether your goal is to write newspaper stories or novels or biographies or publicity releases for a community organization, you will profit by building that same sort of system for yourself.

NEWSTHINKING, THE INNER GAME of newswriting, is a marvelous performance, a testament to the human brain's capacity—and yet it is almost never analyzed. It is one of those achievements regarded as "natural" by those reporters who write well and as "magic" by those who can't.

Whom should we believe? Both sides sound logical: Newswriting is natural, a blend of hundreds of mental and physical steps ordered and monitored by the brain. And it's magic—at least, when you're working at the peak of your game and the words are flowing and the creative impulses are coming out of nowhere and the story writes itself, it seems like magic, right?

Forget it. If you want to keep thinking like that, you're settling for less. You're squandering your talent. You're taking the easy way out.

Because writing—while one of the most complex mental and social acts a human can perform—is nevertheless a definable skill like any other. You improve it by making more efficient use of your inherited attributes. The people who best succeed at increasing their efficiency are those who concentrate the hardest on doing so.

Sadly, among most reporters and editors there is little emphasis on either concentration or improvement of writing . . . and it shows. The quality of writing in the average newspaper remains woeful. It discourages potential readers from delving more deeply into the news and it discourages people with first-rate minds from devoting themselves to news work. They burn out or grow disenchanted too quickly.

To avoid getting caught in that quagmire, you have to begin looking at the world of newswriting in a different way. You have to stop concentrating on merely the *results* of good writing—the examples they show you in most textbooks. You have to begin thinking about the *causes*—the thought strategies that created those polished samples.

To do that, you need a massive injection of vision and imagination. Because the only way to improve your prewriting process—your ability to organize information and make the right choices—is to look inside yourself, to look hard at what you're doing. There is no physical evidence here, no scrapbook of story clippings; instead, you must visualize the stages of mental preparation you now go through, and then begin bolstering them. You must build them into a more thorough, more efficient information-processing system.

EVEN THE LEAST SKILLED REPORTER works according to some kind of subconscious mental formula, some crude, unspoken plan by which he decides how to conduct an interview, what questions to ask, when to take notes, how to use his memory, test his creativity, write his leads. The trouble is, this unskilled reporter has no idea that his mental processes are shallow because he seldom *talks* to another reporter about the inner game. He rarely compares, so he rarely learns.

But we will.

We will show you, for one thing, that the mental development of any story—news, feature, obituary, whatever—follows a general chain of thought. Some of the steps in this cycle of information processing may seem obvious to you, but what's more important is the *unity* among them. The steps—we have about a dozen elemental ones—are an obstacle course that no one ever runs perfectly or without variation. What's so enticing about writing is finding out how close to perfection you can come. As you study the steps, you'll realize that you—and most other working newsmen—are far, far away from your optimum level.

By the time you finish this book, you should be

building your professional skills with goals far higher than those of the average newsman. You should never again have to worry about competing against another reporter, because there will be a new, more challenging target to take aim at—your own potential.

THIS BOOK IS NOT A MIRACLE CURE. It assumes you have or will acquire sound news instincts and a passion for newswriting. Without them, you may build an elaborate, polished mental system but you'll still crank out nothing but well-structured oatmeal. You may turn out to be just what the "happy news" television consultants want, but you won't be a good reporter.

This book wouldn't be needed if so many newspapers—and so many of their reporters—weren't so willing to settle for so little. Pick up any newspaper and examples abound. There's the feature story that was blown because the writer didn't use his heart. The news story with the real news in the ninth paragraph because the writer didn't have the guts to depart from the chronology and define the essence of what he observed. The half-hearted analysis of a local water district audit, so thickly littered with uninterpreted financial details that only an accountant—not the average reader who deals with the district only when he pays his bill—could understand it.

Spread the blame if you want to—the way they teach writing in high school, the way news staffs are kept too thin . . . there are a dozen more excuses if you'd like to fill them in here—but the spotlight inevitably falls on the reporter. He wrote those stories; he blew them. He had the control. He had the power. He had the facts.

And he had the typewriter. What went wrong was inside his head, and if we want to improve the quality of newswriting, we have to start there.

Introduction

TAKE A FEW MINUTES. Look around your own classroom or newsroom and find the best writer. Watch him type. Why is he better? Why, if all of you collected the same information before writing a story, would his be the one that a city editor would run?

The answer lies in the brain. Or, if you wish to use a broader term, in the mind. That skilled reporter's brain has organized the thinking and writing process into a highly efficient series of steps—a far more refined process than the one you use. From there, his brain has learned that basic structure so well that many of the steps begin to come in clusters—he doesn't have to worry about performing them one step at a time.

Remember, we are not talking about his physical capacity; you don't increase the number of muscle fibers in your arms when you do forty push-ups a night—you merely increase the strength and endurance of your existing muscles. In the same way, that reporter has developed his ability to organize a story not by increasing the number of active nerve cells in his brain (adults can't do that), but by improving the extent and subtlety of the nerve cells' interconnections and their readiness to fire.

That's not magic.

But that's why he appears to have a "quick mind," to "jump" several thoughts ahead in crucial situations. His brain has learned to combine a series of steps in his basic composing process without having to monitor the feedback step by step. That's what allows him, for example, to read through a city budget and quickly glean the correct lead, while you move more slowly, not as sure of what you're looking for, lacking that sense of structure between each thought.

That's why he can put more thought into his story than you—and why he can do it in less time.

That's why his stories always feature good transition between paragraphs, while yours keep being rewritten. That's why his stories always seem to provide the correct perspective on an event, while the copydesk. has to do so much inserting in yours. That's why his leads are always crisp and never butchered by the desk. That's why his features are usually bright and creative, as though a separate voice—not the usual bang-bang-bang, hard-news voice—were composing them.

NOW, WHEN WE WALK ACROSS THE ROOM to ask this reporter to explain how he or she does all this, we run into an eighteenth-century German philosopher:

"When the psychical powers are in action," Immanuel Kant says, "one does not observe oneself; and when one observes oneself, those powers stop. A person noticing that someone is watching him and is trying to explore him will either become embarrassed, in which case he *cannot* show himself as he is; or he will disguise himself, in which case he does not *want* to be recognized for what he is."

And so by the time we finish asking that reporter just how it's done, he or she is ready with answers like:

"I dunno, it's just there."

Or: "Some days, it's just hittin'."

Or: "I never know what I think until I see it on paper."

What you're hearing is, "It's magic. I have it, you

don't. Tough luck." We're back to where we started. It's the kind of attitude—even when voiced kindly— that explains why some very good reporters turn out to be mediocre editors: They can't teach because they have never understood their own processes.

REMEMBER, EVEN MAGIC HAS STRUCTURE. Since World War II, psychologists and engineers have been studying human skills, examining people like assembly line workers, executives and athletes in an attempt to answer the misleadingly simple question "How does he or she *do* it?" In each area, they have tried to break down the broad components of a skill that had been largely taken for granted, trying to explain how the brain issues commands to the body and then regulates the action. They have learned the basic techniques man uses to achieve "skilled performance."

One of the most significant conclusions, derived from studies of complex industrial processing operations, is that the skilled operator appears to build a "conceptual framework" or model of the mental and physical processes he is using and the manner in which they function. He uses his imagination to construct a mental picture of the way he does his job. Often, he can't put it into words without a tremendous amount of effort, but that doesn't bother him. All he wants is a standard—a sense of how it should *feel* to do the job the right way, whether it's running a loading dock, assembling part of a DC-10 wing or sorting mail for a Post Office route.

And that's what we're after here: to make you come to grips with your skill, to force you to build and then streamline a model of your writing process, to make you conscious of the need to program your reporter's mind the same way a computer is programmed.

Your central task is the creation of a series of mental "filters," one for each step in your prewriting process. Each time you prepare a story, each decision—each rough outline, each question, each piece of information, each new combination of paragraphs—will be run through several or all of the filters. Depending on how proficient you become, this review may take seconds or long, painful minutes. But it is the only way to aim for greatness. Your filters are your standards, tests of completeness that each fact and impulse must undergo. The order in which you subject your facts to your filters is yours to choose; it is an intimate, personal test. So, ultimately, are the kinds of filters you decide to create. The ones described in the following chapters represent a good starting point, but don't be afraid to augment or change them. What's important is to begin formally developing this kind of process, to *experience* it, to examine it, to know what it feels like when you're working at full blast and to know when you're off, when your system needs to be strengthened—when the sophistication of that computer program inside your head has to be increased.

As the process of subconsciously routing each story through your filters and monitoring the results becomes more automatic, you can begin taking more risks: you can vary your styles of writing, experiment with structure, cram unusual amounts of information into a particular paragraph—all with the confidence that your chain of filters will test the experiment and reject it if it doesn't work.

REMEMBER THE BATTLEFIELD: Newspaper writing is not "Writing." No more than shooting a basketball at your front-yard hoop is like playing in a basketball game with nine others. Or strumming a guitar is like playing in a band in front of three thousand people. "Writer" connotes the sun, reflecting on the forces around it. The reality of "newswriter" is the asteroid, being tugged at violently from every angle—bitchy sources, bitchy competitors, bitchy editors, bitchy readers, deadlines, space limitations and the emotional fragility those pressures create.

You may love it, but that's not enough. You have to consciously define your skills by these pressures. You have to examine your talents and build them with the goal of bringing order out of chaos. Today's newsrooms may offer the quiet of computerized type systems and the coolness of air conditioning, but don't be misled. Mentally, the craft remains etched in noise and sweat and the millions of pieces of news and non-news that have to be handled. Conquer them or they will kill you.

Your newsthinking must be tailored to the reality of news. Your system of newswriting values has to enable you to continually make aggressive choices about the raw data you confront; throw out "bad" (useless) information; keep the "good" and process it through your filters; and invoke rules of flexibility to retrieve any "bad" information, should the circumstances of the news story change.

This is the kind of system that heightens the unity between your newswriting skills and your brain's natural talent for making rapid-fire choices and double-checking the results. It is the kind of system that merges your discipline and creativity, helping them both to function at the richest level.

With this writing process, you judge each piece of information as soon as it arrives. "Does it belong in my story?" you demand to know, the same way your brain and nervous system constantly screen out useless data that would otherwise bombard your senses. The information that qualifies for your story is analyzed and combined by passing through the filters. Choices are continually being made, in much the same way as your brain initiates, monitors and regulates behavior through "yes" and "no" impulses fired by its nerve cells.

DOES THAT SOUND COLD? Does it sound like somebody is thinking about hooking electrodes from your frontal lobes to a video display terminal? Not at all. Your brain is your life. You and your writing are an extension of it. It contains an amazing wealth of power, logic, efficiency and creativity, and the known scope of its resources is growing furiously as neurology and psychology begin to merge.

In the words of Nigel Calder, a British journalist who researched a BBC special on man's understanding of his mind, twentieth-century brain research is like sixteenth-century astronomy: "We are the privileged onlookers in a Copernican phase when men are putting their conscious experience into orbit around the brain. We may be waiting for the Isaac Newton of the nervous system who will reveal what holds this (mental) universe together."

Even in a profession as finite as ours, you have a stake in such lofty perspective. New discoveries by brain and mind researchers have helped us to define the structure of our magic and our potential to improve it. In just the past few years, for example, a kind of cult has built up around the study of the right cerebral hemisphere of the brain. Understand: you have two cerebral hemispheres, often performing widely different functions. The left side handles speech and numbers and perceives the world strictly by the chronology in which events happen. The right side is "holistic"—it expresses itself by nonverbal, subjective, intuitive impulses and allows you to understand relationships between parts and wholes.

Applied to newswriting, the increasingly popular right-hemisphere theory maintains that when a reporter writes a good feature story, he uses the right half of his brain to develop a creative angle. He then "shifts" to his left hemisphere, using it to convert that angle into words and analyze the results, then moves back to the right side for further inspiration, then back to the left side to check it out, and so on.

IS THAT WHAT REALLY HAPPENS in your brain? Can you control it? Scientific opinion is mixed, but the separate talents of the dual hemispheres are clear—the potential is there. Why wait for science to catch up if *envisioning* that kind of back-and-forth process between your logical and emotional sides helps you write better features?

That's the cutting edge: The more clearly you perceive the way your mind collects, shuffles, reshuffles, retrieves and then spits out the components of your stories, the more you'll write with perspective, authority and speed. You'll do it because you'll *feel*, subtly, the chaotic flood of ideas narrowing into a line of thought that will suddenly race from your head to your fingers and produce the story. You'll know something about why it happens, and you'll know something about how to make it happen more often.

The chapters that follow are organized by their importance in the prewriting process and not necessarily by the sequence in which you will use them. Part of the agony and wonderment of newswriting is that nobody can predict the order in which these steps will come into play—it differs every time you start working on a new story. Diagram I.1 presents one order in an attempt to illustrate how the chapters in this book relate to one another.

Each individual's strengths and weaknesses will dictate which stages he needs to concentrate on more. Some reporters who have had trouble writing feature stories may ultimately find the "creativity" filter their most important one. Others may rely most heavily on the "self-editing" filter, which is aimed at improving your copy once it's written. But these are refinements, and they cannot be fully exploited without the primary building blocks.

BRIEFLY, HERE'S WHERE WE'RE GOING: Chapters 1 and 2 explain how to tailor your mind to confront the mass of information that litters each story's trail. First, we'll examine the brain's basic command structure. You have to start here to develop more confidence in your ability to make quick, accurate decisions in sorting out facts and mastering the most savage of newswriting tasks. Then we'll work on attitude, on developing the arrogant stance needed when you begin sifting information.

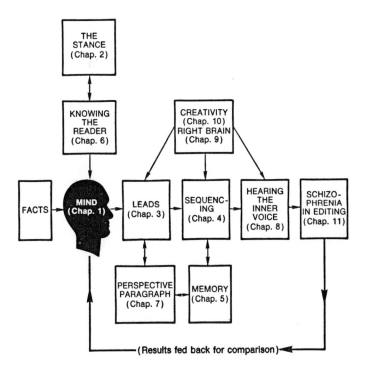

Diagram I.1. One order in which a story can be processed through a reporter's mental filters.

Next come three chapters on key fundamental thought strategies that come into play as you move closer to typing. Chapter 3 will illustrate the construction of a mental filter to test your lead paragraphs. Chapter 4 will deal with the development of a "sequencing" filter, which will monitor whether all of the story's facts have been put in proper sequence. And Chapter 5 will help you build a filter that asks whether you have called on your memory.

From there, in Chapters 6 through 11, we will concentrate on supplemental filters that will force you to continually ask yourself whether you have made the story relevant to the reader (Chapter 6); whether you have supplied the proper factual perspective (Chapter 7); whether you have made good use of your "inner voice" in composing the story (Chapter 8); whether you have pushed your creative resources hard enough (Chapters 9 and 10); and whether you have remembered to edit your own copy carefully (Chapter 11).

Finally, in Chapter 12, we'll discuss the impact of pressure—an ever-present enemy in newsrooms—on your work.

Before we begin, however, a bit of guidance:

Rule Number 1:
There Are No Rules.

IF YOU REMEMBER NOTHING ELSE, remember Rule Number 1. It is a joyful tribute to the fact that no two news stories or circumstances are the same, that each reporter has to make his own decisions, has to be in control of his own story. When talented people work together, they eventually wind up throwing out all policies except Rule Number 1.

News operations that disregard this rule take on the collective mentality of the golfing gorilla: A man approaches the first tee and sees his friend is waiting with his clubs—and a gorilla. The gorilla plays golf, he explains, putting a driver in the animal's hands and positioning it. The gorilla swings and hits a perfect shot, 280 yards down the fairway. The ball stops 15 feet from the hole. When the party arrives for the second shot, the man hands the gorilla a putter. The gorilla swings and hits the ball 280 yards again.

The gorilla's human counterpart is the reporter who does a heart-wrenching, two-hour interview with a family whose child is battling a fatal illness, then comes back to the office and writes fifteen inches because two days ago the assistant city editor told him his piece on a fund-raising event was too long.

Rule Number 1 makes it clear that if any rules or policies have to exist, they can be broken—crushed—whenever the news requires it. The business is too unpredictable for anyone to say "I will *never . . .* " Rule Number 1 symbolizes the kind of thinking that keeps newspapers vibrant, living entities. It stands flatly against the breed of publishers and editors who use words like "product" to describe what they put out.

Use that rule while you read this book. Some of its ideas will work for you. Some may trigger new insights. Others may fall flat. Please, don't be too rigid. Don't simply accept one author's description of the way a newswriter's mental system works or feels. Building a conceptual framework of your own process is an asset only if it comes from your soul. Your kind of mental filters may feel completely different from mine. You may visualize their operation as doggy doors or windows, through which your stories are processed in the forms of poodles or flies. No matter. Does it help? Then do it.

For the most uninhibited approach to improving the

efficiency of your reporter's mind, remember this: There is no consensus in the scientific community about what's going on "up there." Psychologists, neurologists, physiologists—their fields are still separated by generations of rivalry and disparate terminology. And even within each specialty, experts continue to promote competing theories. So you needn't worry about conforming to any doctrines in building a conceptual model of your writing process.

The model does not have to be scientifically proven, but it does have to be built. In the following chapter we begin to lay the foundation.

1.

What's Up There?

STEEL YOURSELF. Concentrate. This is the toughest chapter. No gimmicks to ease the pressure. I want you to think about your brain.

Here's why: To succeed as a newswriter, you have to create a newswriting *attitude* that consciously models your skills after the brain's ability to confront huge amounts of information (sensory data), select what's necessary and put it in the proper perspective. In both the healthy, active brain and the healthy, active writing system, the result of this process is the same: an accurate portrait of the world around you. The best newswriters are those whose writing processes are the most direct extensions of their brains' logic and efficiency.

A generation ago, this concept could have been dismissed as useless (by newspaper editors) and invalid (by scientists). Newspapers operated in a far more structured world. Reporters had less information to deal with and, more important, spent a far greater percentage of their time on predictable, institutionalized stories. Beats were less complicated. The sources for an average story were fewer in number. Fuzzy concepts like "lifestyle" and "social upheaval" were still regarded as the exclusive property of sociologists. There was far less intensive investigative reporting. There were no 300-page "environmental impact reports." The typical reporter did not have to make anywhere near as many difficult choices about what to write—and what to leave out—as he does today. His writing process, and his brain, didn't have to be as aggressive.

This state of affairs corresponded nicely with the views of most brain researchers and theorists of a generation ago: to them, the brain was a far less active organ than the one we now know. Science was largely content to view the brain as a series of passive responding devices whose actions were determined by the stimuli arriving from the outside world. Questions about how the brain might initiate or plan human behavior were relatively rare.

But back in the newsroom, things were about to change. The society that had been comfortably covered in the past was beginning to explode in a torrent of complexity; the diversity of life, work and attitudes in the sixties and seventies was mushrooming at a pace no one was prepared for. The changes strained the resilience—and the good judgment—of even the most flexible editors.

It was like "ten Industrial Revolutions and Protestant Reformations all rolled into one and all taking place in a single generation," said John Platt, associate director of the University of Michigan's Mental Health Research Institute.

He was talking about a series of "watershed reversals" compressed into little more than a decade: East-West détente, the ecology movement, the falling U.S. birth rate, the women's movement, the shift in world energy supplies, changes in racial and sexual tolerance, legal and religious reforms, consumerism.

TO REPORTERS, THE CHALLENGE IS THIS: Sharpen your mind's ability to stratify and interpret what you see, or you're worthless. Reporters who fail to do this—who continue to envision their minds as simply big "in" baskets—are finding themselves bypassing or squandering stories about complicated issues. There remain hundreds of news niches where you can get by that way, but not forever. No good reporter can expect to work in the 1980s and beyond without consciously developing an aggressive information-processing system.

Interestingly, most theorists now agree you have a brain that can function exactly that way. Just as we in news refuse to tolerate the notion that a reporter's job is merely to respond to information that comes into the office, so has science discredited the idea that human behavior is merely a response to stimuli. We now know that behavior is active in character, and that the brain determines activity not only by past experience but also by plans and designs that formulate the future.

However, we are still far away from understanding exactly what goes on amid the nerve cells and chemical encounters that launch our brains into action. Consider, for example, the irony of this lead sentence from a book review in a brain-research publication:

How the Brain Works, by Leslie A. Hart (Basic Books, $10.50), needless to say does not tell how the brain works . . . .

Most of us are discouraged from coming to grips with our brains because of their intricacy. Indeed, we're put off even by this peripheral question: How are our brains and bodies able to combine in the myriad of skills we take for granted? Yet questions like that have been asked in America since 1897, when a pair of researchers named Bryan and Harter began investigating the twin skills of Morse key tapping and typewriting. They wondered what the nature of brain organization must be that enabled a telegraph operator to so rapidly and accurately decode the response. How could a train dispatcher do so many things almost simultaneously—record train movement, figure a special meeting point, double-check reports from other stations and factor numerous variables (weather, weight of trains, delays) into his calculations?

Not surprisingly, the researchers were able to describe far more than they were able to explain. Even today, not much is known about the neurological mechanisms that make our muscles do what we expect of them.

One reason for this void is that scientific ethics does not allow healthy men and women to be subjected to the kind of brain experiments performed on animals. So virtually everything we know has been learned from work on patients with abnormal brains, through examination of brain damage, experiments with drugs, and brain surgery. Enough has been learned to create models of some basic functions—language, for example—and illustrate how various brain areas work.

FOR A ROUGH IDEA, let's go back to the newsroom, where you're making your fourth telephone call in the last ten minutes. You're trying to dig up the address of a local pilot whose airliner just crashed. Finally, you score. The sheriff's deputy on the other end reads the information: 1876 Bedford Street.

The numbers and street name enter your ear, and the machinery of the inner ear converts a jumbled pattern of sound waves into a coded signal to be sent to the brain. The audible difference between Bedford Street and Medford Street is slim, but your hearing mechanism quickly makes the distinction and sends the message.

The coded signal goes to the left temporal (side) lobe of the brain, the critical area for the recognition of words.

To make sure the impulses that eventually reach your fingers are correct, the signal is now sent to at least three other regions of the brain. One of these areas, located high up and toward the back of the brain, provides the ability to shape letters correctly. A second, low in the left of the brain and toward the front, is in charge of putting letters and words together in the correct order. Finally, the signal is processed by the brain's frontal lobes, the little-understood region that is thought to be responsible for programming and planning.

After that, the signal is routed to the brain's motor strip, another region in the roof of the brain, which has control of the muscles that produce movement. At various points along the motor strip, each part of the body is represented. For you to write down 1876 Bedford Street, specific nerve cells in the motor strip, assigned to control each of your fingers, fire off instructions to the required muscles. The signal is transferred to paper.

The entire process seems to happen instantly. Anyway, you're too busy to think about it—that address was the last piece of information you needed for your plane crash story. Now you swivel your chair to face the keyboard, and as you begin typing the story, you realize it's one of those days. One of those good days. It's as though your fingers are wired to the keys; the impulses—the paragraphs—shoot out one after another, as though an electric charge were running down your arms from your brain, carrying the prolific explosion of words from your head.

Certainly there's a case for calling that description fantasy. (Especially if you're using a manual typewriter.) But always strive for that feeling of electrical unity. Believe (or pretend, if you have to) that the story is a stream of energy surging from your brain to the copy paper or VDT screen.

Because in a very real sense, your brain is making its decisions and dictating its commands through electric impulses. It has been known for more than 150 years that electricity is involved in the interaction of nerves and muscles. By the middle of the nineteenth century, scientists discovered that the brain has electric potential, and in 1929 an Austrian doctor, Hans Berger, finally developed a device—the electroencephalograph (EEG)—to register brain waves.

BUT THE BRAIN IS NOT MERELY an electrical machine. It is also a chemical one. A few years before the EEG was developed, researchers began proving that one nerve cell in the brain influences the action of another not by direct electrical connection, but by sending a chemical "transmitter substance" into a tiny gap that separates the two cells.

Every piece of information the world sends us through our sense organs—every thought, action and feeling—must be coded into the language of the nerve cell, or *neuron*. The magic of the brain lies in the way each neuron connects with the others. Each receives information from other neurons or from sensory receptors, and transmits information to still other neurons or to muscles, glands and other departments of the body. That's what produces behavior.

Within the brain, neurons communicate mainly with each other. They are jammed together like the wiring of the most complex computer imaginable—there are about 10,000 million neurons in the roof of the brain alone. The branches at the transmitting ends are connected to other neurons by sticky pads. The junction where they meet—perhaps a millionth of an inch of room—is called a *synapse*. It is across the synapse that signals are passed from one neuron to another by the release of a transmitter substance.

Think back for a moment to the outside world of your work. In newsthinking, the goal is to build the most efficient and vigilant system of making choices about the information you confront. If you want to know where that ability comes from, look to your brain. It not only provides that skill, it personifies it. It builds an intelligent choice out of an endless number of neurons and electrical impulses.

HERE, IN AN OVERSIMPLIFIED WAY, is how: Each neuron and each synapse is essentially constant in character. Each neuron is either *excitatory* (whenever it fires, it encourages the firing of the next neuron) or *inhibitory* (its firing discourages the second from firing). Synapses are similarly classified: a neuron fired through an excitatory synapse will encourage the firing of another neuron; a neuron fired through an inhibitory synapse will discourage the neuron on the other side. And so the logic of your brain's circuits is shaped.

The crucial questions—Should the neuron extend the sensory impulse? Should the message be carried further?—occur at the synaptic junction. What happens there is best explained by the political analogy of journalist Nigel Calder in his fine introduction to contemporary brain research, *Mind of Man*:

> A neuron in action is like a delegate meeting. On a particular issue, the meeting can collectively decide "yes" or "no" or do nothing. "Doing nothing," for a neuron, often means ticking over quietly, firing several times each second. At a "yes" vote, the neuron fires much more rapidly; at a "no" vote, its casual firing is suppressed.
>
> There are typically some hundreds of delegates at this meeting, sitting 'round the edge of the neuron; they are the synapses, each representing another neuron. Some of these delegates are well known for their tendency to vote "yes," for they are the excitatory synapses, representative of the radical neurons. Others are conservatives (inhibitory synapses), tending to vote "no." All are under instructions from their own neurons, though, and in a particular vote many synapses may abstain. The outcome—whether the neuron in question fires more rapidly or slowly—is democratically determined by comparing the votes of the two factions.

As in most political interplay, there is a trend here, leading us to an important analogy between the way the human brain works and the way your newsthinking should be refined.

The combined vote of the synapses usually turns out to be a conservative one. By being biased against firing neurons, the brain responds only to necessary information. You should be building your reporting skills on that kind of philosophy: exploiting your inhibitory powers, developing instincts that tell you what to chase and what to leave alone, increasing your ability to get to the heart of a story without being sidetracked, shutting out surrounding chaos. Your success in achieving this discipline depends on the kinds of attitudes we'll describe in Chapter 2. For the moment, simply appreciate the fact that you're able to function on this planet only because your brain sets up standards and rules. It does not treat all facts equally. If it did—by firing neurons in response to all stimuli—"you'd have an epileptic fit every time you opened your eyes," one brain researcher suggests.

THE BRAIN ADOPTS A STRATEGY, as the child playing checkers adopts a strategy, allowing him to select a sensible move every few seconds. Without a strategy—without standards—he would feel pressured to calculate every conceivable consequence of every legitimate move.

The reporter, faced with the same type of endless-choice dilemma, must likewise perfect his own strategies. In the chapter that follows, you will learn to plot yours.

2.

Your Stance

No wind favors him who has no destined port.

—Michel de Montaigne,
sixteenth-century
French essayist

SEE IF THIS SOUNDS FAMILIAR. You're waiting to interview someone and his secretary asks you, "What's your angle? How are you writing this?"

And you answer, "I don't know yet. I'm just trying to find out what's happening."

You're lying. To the secretary and—whether or not you realize it—to yourself.

Editors relentlessly insist that reporters walk into each new assignment with no preconceptions. What's ironic—and what most editors never mention—is that the best reporters purposely begin shaping biases as soon as they begin gathering facts on a particular assignment. This is part of their response to the staggering complexity of the world they have to cover. To succeed, they have developed a more sophisticated information-processing system, one that takes fullest advantage of the human brain's natural ability to organize. The care they have used in building this system is what allows them to squeeze out every drop of their talent.

It's vital to understand how a skilled reporter focuses his powers of attention—how he listens and reads. His ability to string words together and organize facts on paper will be crippled if he does not psych himself into the correct attitude—the proper "stance"—for the gathering of information.

The skilled reporter is aware that his mind can successfully process only a certain amount of data. To compensate for that limitation he assumes a mental posture of arrogance. He virtually dares any source to provide him with usable information. On the outside, he may appear to have the patience of a saint, but inside his attitude toward extraneous information is harsh.

At the start of each coverage situation, to help himself look for the kind of information he needs, he begins building a running mental hypothesis—a crude outline, a sense of where the story is headed. Each piece of new information either helps confirm that hypothesis or persuades the reporter to modify his impression of the story as a whole.

This interplay between new data and a perceptual framework is a prime link in any skilled performance, from writing to bicycle riding. The most efficient performer has developed the fastest and most accurate system of what psychologists sometimes call *perceptual coding*.

The relationship between this natural ability and your own newswriting is clear: Be more conscious of sorting—"coding"—the information you collect as a reporter, and your ability to handle larger amounts of complex facts will improve.

Like many mental functions, perceptual coding is so obvious that its importance is often overlooked. Your brain groups and orders all data it confronts: Working through a still-mysterious filter that seems to protect its systems against overload, the brain takes new sensory information and links it to material stored in the memory. That puts the new data in perspective, setting the stage for action based on the new perception.

Your eyes are an example. What they see is merely an undefined collection of objects, but your visual system works with the brain to interpret the fragments and turn them into a coherent picture.

ALMOST SUBCONSCIOUSLY, THE BEST reporters work the same way, always seeing the story in perspective. They build the frameworks of their stories—hypotheses—as soon as they begin working on them, comparing each new piece of information to the framework. In that way, they're able to keep their overall goal in sight, ask better questions, react more sharply to surprise answers and constantly organize their information. Average reporters, on the other hand, often operate as little more than data collectors, and don't begin putting the information in perspective until they're driving back to the office or sitting down at the typewriter.

By then it's often too late.

Remember, though, that he who lives by the framework can also die by it. To set up a story framework, you have to create a number of biases— temporary mental prejudices—against unrelated information. If you have made a mistake in your hypothesis, you will be perceiving your facts incorrectly, or looking for the wrong ones.

A skilled reporter avoids this pitfall by exploiting a parallel ability: acute sensitivity to any piece of information that contradicts his running hypothesis. He can set up a story framework early in the fact-gathering process because he is confident of his ability to adjust the framework in response to new evidence.

This process usually goes on with only the slightest external clues. A reporter who has mastered it may "feel" the story falling into place, but he rarely has the time to actively concentrate on whether each new piece of information confirms or modifies his hypothesis. He's too busy devoting most of his attention to asking a question or writing down an answer.

So don't be fooled by appearances. A reporter whose

interview or research style looks disjointed may have organized his internal information-processing system superbly. That's what allows him to take more chances, ask more questions, grab at more straws during an interview—knowing all the while that his subconscious is meticulously sifting things. Ask him how he puts complicated stories in order and he may start talking about "good instincts."

Code word: "magic." My advice to you: Don't buy it.

YOU CANNOT THROW A SWITCH in your mind and suddenly possess the sophisticated attention mechanism of a skilled reporter. But you can, over a period of time, improve your mental process.

For example, examine how you use your powers of attention while you research or interview. How do you divide your attention between the piece of information you're looking at and the overall picture—the story framework?

This is the kind of issue—the kind of thought strategy—that most reporters never tackle. They're too overwhelmed or uninspired by the job to look inside themselves and consider what portions of their energy are reserved for various mental tasks—and how they might improve. They consider a skill such as the power of attention to be much the same as the color of their eyes—a constant. It's not.

To control these kinds of variables, you begin slowly. You concentrate for months. You set a goal. For example, in interview situations the finest reporters are able to devote 90 percent of their attention to the question at hand, requiring only the remaining 10 percent to place that new information in perspective. Can you perform at that level automatically? Probably not. Chances are you usually have to put more effort into that latter chore—into figuring where your next question is coming from, into strengthening the links between incoming information from the interview subject and the storehouse of information in your memory.

To improve, concentrate at first on equally dividing your consciousness—50 percent to what you're hearing at the moment, 50 percent to asking yourself the supplementary question, How does this new information fit into the story?

Gradually, you should need less of your mind to perform the perspective function.

While newspaper reporting is not a profession—it's a craft, like making leather sandals—there are times when the level of required skill is as high as that of any of the so-called professions. This process of quickly comparing each fact to the big picture is one of them. Here the reporter works with the same sharp-edged intensity as the biochemist hunched over a microscope, instinctively weighing each fact against his running hypothesis. One piece of information tends to confirm it; another modifies it; yet another triggers the need for more evidence.

THINK ABOUT THIS KIND OF SKILL the next time you observe in action a reporter whose writing you admire. Watch him ask questions. Note his ability to interpret subtle shifts in the tone and direction of an interview or research, and to respond immediately—either by modifying his hypothesis or leaning on the source.

Often, the source will want to change the subject prematurely; the skilled reporter senses that it's not time because his running hypothesis still seems valid and his need for evidence to confirm it remains unsatisfied.

For an example of what this process looks like when it works—and when it doesn't—we take you to police headquarters. We are watching the reporter, Mr. Mitchell, interview the local police chief, Captain Hendrix. In observing Mitchell, we will see that he has either an unsatisfactory grasp of where he wants the interview to go, or an insufficient amount of guts to raise a decent follow-up question:

MITCHELL: Let's talk about the police shootings. Officers killed sixteen suspects in the past year—twice as many as the year before—and the police commission last month approved a stricter policy on when an officer can fire his gun. How will officers adjust, and what's your feeling about the new policy?

HENDRIX: We're cops, and we know the commission is the head of the department. We know the rules. We'll follow them. We'll probably respond by holding a training seminar for all our officers.

MITCHELL: When will that be?

HENDRIX: In about a month. I feel it's important

for each officer to know the changes that have come down, in terms of policy—

Wait a minute, Mitchell. Does the chief of police agree with the new shooting policy or doesn't he? In the back of Mitchell's mind (no neurological significance intended), a red light or siren should have gone off as soon as Hendrix began talking about compliance with the policy. The reporter should have been operating with a story framework that featured a big slot labeled "Chief's Opinion." And when it became obvious the chief would rather not give his opinion, Mitchell's subconscious mind should have reminded his conscious mind that the void in the framework remained. He should have responded.

It should have happened like this:

HENDRIX: We're cops, and we know the commission is the head of the department. We know the rules. We'll follow them. We'll probably respond by holding a training seminar for all our officers.

MITCHELL: Let me ask you specifically: Do you like the new shooting policy?

HENDRIX: Well, I think it demands too much of an officer and sets a standard of conduct that I'm not too certain he can comply with.

MITCHELL: It's too harsh?

HENDRIX: Yes, it's too harsh.

MITCHELL: Why?

Let's hand the interview back to Mitchell at this point and see what he makes of it. Chief Hendrix answers the question about why the new shooting policy is too harsh:

HENDRIX: Police officers get paid to do a job. They are not robots. They are not perfect. If you look at our record of shootings over the past five years, you can see that.

MITCHELL: What were the numbers?

HENDRIX: Well, you mentioned there were sixteen in '77 and eight in '76. In 1975, there were—

TOO BAD. Our reporter lost him again because his mind didn't flash a warning signal when the chief offered only a vague, emotional reason for his dislike of the new policy. That slot in the story framework, "Chief's Opinion," needs fleshing out the way any other opinion does. A complete "why" is as important as "yes" or "no." When Mitchell heard the generalized answer to his question about why the new policy was too harsh, he should have felt the tug of his story's framework. The void had still not been completely taken care of. He should have trusted his memory to come back for the statistics of the past five years later in the interview. He should not have let the chief slip away. Something like this should have taken place:

HENDRIX: Yes, it's too harsh.

MITCHELL: Why?

HENDRIX: Police officers get paid to do a job. They are not robots. They are not perfect. If you look at our record of shootings over the past five years, you can see that.

MITCHELL: I want to make sure I understand what you're saying. Specifically, show me how an officer *can't* do his job just as well while conforming to the new policy.

HENDRIX: Well, take a fleeing felon. The new policy says we cannot shoot him. I believe if an officer has seen the felony suspect commit the act in question, and makes a persistent, audible demand for him to halt, and the suspect does not, then the officer should be allowed to fire with intent only to wound. Without that prerogative, I fear for the safety of those whom that fleeing felon may next attack . . . .

A better internal sense of where the story was going—the ability to see the story as a whole—would have allowed reporter Mitchell to ask questions that produced those two key answers: (1) The chief doesn't like the new policy. (2) He's worried about additional crime as a result of it. Perhaps Mitchell would have run into those observations by accident later in the interview—but not if the chief didn't want him to. Clearly, the source, not the reporter, was in control of that interview.

Here is a personal consequence of failing to work from a story framework: The U.S. congressman who represented my newspaper's district died unexpectedly, and in putting together the story I made a few phone calls seeking comments from his close political associates. One call went to a local state senator. While we were chatting, I asked if he knew the time frame for the governor to call a special election to fill the remainder of the congressman's term. The senator knew the procedure in fine detail. I thanked him and turned to my other calls. A half hour later he called me back and said, "Say, you didn't ask me about this, but I thought you'd be interested: I'll probably run for that seat."

Now, how could I have forgotten to ask him whether he would run? By working on a story at a scattershot pace, by telling myself that I'd "put it all together" as soon as I'd made the last call, that's how. If I had been concentrating, I would have begun shaping a story framework in my mind as soon as I began making the calls, as illustrated by Diagram 2.1. A big fat space

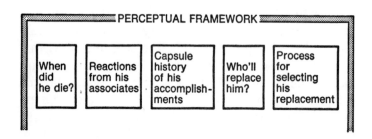

Diagram 2.1. In this story, a prominent congressman has died unexpectedly. As the reporter begins gathering information, broad, primary issues in the story are first organized in this fashion, with each issue given a crude title and then cataloged—but not in any order of importance. This creates a rough guide to help the reporter search for relevant facts.

would have been set aside in the framework for the obvious question, Who'll Replace Him? The minute the state senator started rattling off the election procedure so precisely, that slot in the framework would have tugged on my attention. I would have been forced to ask myself, Why does *this* guy know so much about the dates? Why else?

MEET THE NASTY LITTLE MAN. We used the word *arrogance* earlier in describing the attitude a reporter must take in a news world glutted with information. Don't forget it. That's your stance: arrogance motivated by confidence. You know why you're covering this particular story; you know what information is likely to be significant; and you know you have only so much time and newspaper space.

In a business in which everybody wants your ear, you have to take the initiative. You have to take the offensive. You have to play the news, or else it will play you. Outwardly, be as polite or naive or condescending or humble as your purposes demand, but inside your gut there has to be a nasty little man (about 5'2" with a goatee, too much nostril hair and a British accent) eternally imploring each source, "Get to the *point,* man. Come *on* with it! Oh, *that's* not important . . . ."

Your little man must personify that arrogance. He is the keeper of the door that leads to your mental shelves.

SHELVES? The image is not important; the concept is. Your ability to construct a story framework has solved some problems. It has allowed you to mentally keep the entire story in front of you, rather than dealing with isolated facts, as you interview or do research. It has helped you decide what to look for, but it has not resolved the next consideration: How do you handle the information you find?

You don't simply begin writing the story. Subconsciously, each reporter uses some sort of mental trick—sometimes crude, sometimes refined—to mentally stack the incoming facts in the order he plans to use them. He must begin doing this as soon as he encounters any new information. If he waits until he begins to write, he's dead.

The construction of a story framework can be envisioned as the placement of the anticipated prime facts in a horizontal line. No priorities are set; the reporter is merely making a mental list of the facts he thinks he will have to gather.

But once he begins collecting those prime facts, decisions have to be made. He arranges the material in what can be thought of as a rough vertical pattern: good stuff on top, bad stuff on the bottom.

There is no prescribed method for this sort of mind game, but at the same time there is no way a reporter can put together a complicated story without going through such a prewriting process—consciously or otherwise. The earlier he begins stacking his facts in his mind, the better off he will be.

The variables in this process are endless, and you should examine your own. Can you assign different facts to different levels or categories in your mind? Do you feel able to shift facts from one level to another if new developments occur? Do you find your own process working more keenly when you are suddenly snowed under with information—say, at a city council hearing when a batch of government reports and public speakers all converge on the same issue?

Sure, you take notes, but your head is what usually holds the broad outline of the story. How well do you organize the information that flows in?

Here's one method, modeled loosely on a technique I found myself using subconsciously after a number of years as a reporter (see Diagram 2.2).

There is an initial "yes/no" filter somewhere in my mind, or so I pretend. It screens each piece of new information to see whether it fits into the story that is

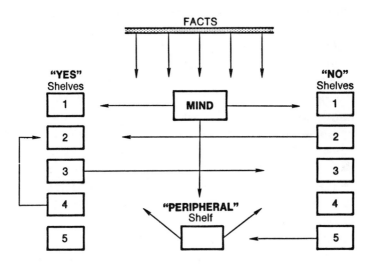

Diagram 2.2. As individual facts are collected, the reporter makes a quick, initial determination of the relevance of each one. Is the information usable or not? Roughly, what is its priority? Subsequent facts may force changes in the position of facts that have been stacked in one of three sets of mental shelves—"Yes," "No," and "Peripheral."

developing. "Yes" material—facts, quotes or other data that seem to have a chance of helping the story—goes to one of several shelves in a "yes" column. The top "yes" shelf is the most important one; I have tried to wipe it clean so that prime facts for only this story will be placed there.

The other "yes" shelves hold lower-priority information, in descending order of importance. Standing parallel to the "yes" shelves are the "no" shelves; most "no" information—data judged to be irrelevant to the story—is stacked here. I do not pay attention to it, although I know that most of it will make its way into my long-term memory, and that some of it will pop back into my consciousness in the future.

Some information I receive doesn't scream out for a particular shelf in my mind, so it is assigned to a shelf standing between the "yes" and "no" columns, a "peripheral" shelf. New circumstances may require information from this shelf to be retrieved and compared with facts on the "yes" or "no" shelves, and possibly to be moved onto one of those shelves.

YOUR MENTAL FILING SYSTEM must be flexible. It does not have to be used with equal intensity in all coverage situations. But it must be ready. Only a reporter with a well-organized mind can master a story in which a fascinating twist of events or unusual human drama is shrouded by complex circumstances. The average reporter is not mentally equipped for such an expedition.

How literally should you try to use this filing system? To the extent that it helps you. How much can you influence it? Plenty. Take the peripheral shelf. What's important here is to exploit background or semi-related information to the fullest degree. When you get an assignment, it is mandatory that you put your peripheral shelf in good order by checking your memory and your paper's library to see if there is relevant background information available. This can be done before you begin building your story framework, and from there a chain reaction takes place: A better framework helps you ask better questions; better questions produce better information to file on your mental shelves.

Like most good ideas, mental organization is an old one. Seventeenth-century scientist-philosopher René Descartes likened the mind to a room, and pointed out that it could be neat or untidy. Obviously, you can find things much more easily in a well-ordered room.

If you're patient enough to push through the wordy translation of Descartes's "Rules for the Direction of the Mind," you can develop a feeling for the kind of mental organization he advocated:

> If I have first found out by separate mental operations what the relation is between the magnitudes A and B, then between B and C, between C and D, and finally between D and E—that does not entail my seeing what the relation is between A and E. Nor can the truths previously learned give me a precise knowledge of it unless I recall them all.
>
> To remedy this, I would run them over from time to time, keeping the imagination moving continuously in such a way that while it is intuitively perceiving each fact, it simultaneously

passes on to the next. This I would do until I had learned to pass from the first to the last so quickly that no stage in the process was left to the care of the memory. [Instead] I seemed to have the whole in intuition before me at the same time. This method will relieve memory, diminish the sluggishness of our thinking, and definitely enlarge our mental capacity.

PSYCH YOURSELF into the necessary state of concentration. Conceive of your attention as a beam of light, which can be focused as sharply as needed upon incoming information; or envision your mind as a computer, neatly processing each new fact through rigid news standards, then flipping each fact like a punch card into a precise mental slot, to be retrieved when circumstances dictate; or picture your progress by telling yourself that improved mental organization is allowing the neurons in your brain to fire correct decisions more quickly than before.

Have an image, and remember: It doesn't do any good to have your typewriter greased up and ready to go unless you have kept your shelves tidy.

Now, step inside the newsroom, where we'll watch an artist at work on one of the most basic mental filters—the "lead" filter.

3.

Leads

MEET MS. TURNER. She is a fictitious character who will appear in our newsroom from time to time to illustrate how newsthinking strategies are put to work. Her attributes symbolize the level of performance we want to shoot for.

Ms. Turner is, among other things, a merchant of leads—the crisp opening paragraphs of a breaking story, the unexpected, twisting, graph-to-graph dance that opens a feature, the heartbreaking ache that introduces the sob story. She's the one everybody in the office seems to seek out at one time or another with a story they can't solve, a story that seems to defy a clever or sensitive lead—and she always seems to deliver. As a result, she's regarded as sort of a doctor of words, but she's really more of a mechanic. Her genius in constructing lead paragraphs lies in her ability to grasp the structure of a story—to take it apart and put it back together, to see how the parts form the whole. She compares the elements that make the story newsworthy; analyzes their importance; mentally extracts the essence of the story; and then translates that impression into words.

Our description of how she does it is going to sound complex, but like any skilled performer, Ms. Turner has taught her brain to make clusters of mental movements rather than one decision at a time. Sometimes a lead may come to her in ten seconds; other times it may take ten minutes, or perhaps two hours of frustrated thinking. Regardless, she subconsciously runs each lead through the same mental process, and then compares her results with her original concept of what the lead paragraphs should accomplish.

In doing that, she is utilizing our system of mental filters—checkpoints along the route that each story travels through her mind. In Chapter 2, we saw how a skilled reporter sets up a "stance" filter to evaluate and organize incoming information. In this chapter, we will construct the first of many mental filters that come into play when you compose your story.

The "lead" filter will force every lead to pass a series of tough tests—and it will force you to begin rewriting if the lead doesn't pass them.

(The order in which a reporter's mind operates is always subject to change. In some instances, he establishes the sequence of the entire story and then concentrates on the lead. In other cases, the process is reversed. We'll work under the latter assumption, and will study sequencing of the overall story in Chapter 4.)

Now, back to Ms. Turner. No matter what kind of story she's trying to write, her goals in shaping the lead are constant. The broadest one: She wants to feel herself closing the gap between the essence of what she knows (her thoughts) and the lead that will appear on paper (her words). She envisions the creation of an image (the lead) that will slide precisely over the essence; writing matched perfectly to reality. She doesn't kid herself. She knows this is not always possible.

Before she begins composing, she analyzes the story elements she collected earlier. Her memory runs over the prime facts. It also reviews the story framework she employed during the information-gathering process. The framework kept her conscious of where the story was heading; now her analysis prompts her to ask, Where has the story wound up? How has it evolved?

HER ABILITY TO SEE PARTS and wholes has taught her that nearly all stories share certain characteristics. For example:

- Conflict: people against each other; people against a system; a person in conflict with his beliefs, having to make a difficult decision; people in conflict with events beyond their control.
- Impact upon her readers. It can be direct (property assessments are up 30 percent) or indirect (the high crime rate is cutting tourism).
- Purely interesting information: silly, warm, dramatic, pathetic, unique. The intensity of these non-conflict, non-impact elements is a key to any good feature story.

Ms. Turner examines her prime facts to find where each of these and other characteristics surfaces. She tries to develop a sense of how much of a role each characteristic plays in this story. Which surfaces most frequently? Which offers the most power? Which characteristic best represents the essence of the story? Which best ties in with her goals for this story?

She never anticipates black-and-white answers to these questions. She often expects to find merely an impulse, rather than a strategy she could put into words. She is simply taking advantage of her finely tuned mind—in effect, hitting a mental trigger that launches a myriad of alternatives. Sometimes the facts are easy to handle and her choice of leads is obvious and instantaneous. Other times, she plays the alternatives against each other, waiting for an angle to pop out, as though the collision between the merging facts and her own news values will somehow force the correct choice into the open.

Finally, the angle comes. She knows the direction her lead will take. Now she composes it word by word, in her head or on the keyboard, and the process of feedback begins. She compares the lead with those original goals: Why is the story being written, and for whom? How successfully does the lead represent the essence of the story? If the lead is indirect (for example, a narrative), how well does it draw the reader into the essence?

Now comes a complex, internal juggling act which has been built and refined thousands of times by years of trial and error. Turner cannot describe this stage very well verbally, but inside she knows when it's clicking. It allows her to rapidly weigh the value of each element in her lead; to ponder which ones may have to be sacrificed or changed; to shuffle the elements around to form new combinations; and, finally, to make her choices. Maybe the first lead she thought of was the right one. Maybe another version works better. Maybe none of them do, forcing her to start over. If the feedback she gets from putting the lead through her filter is positive, she continues to compose the remainder of the story. If she receives negative feedback, she goes back to square one.

DOES THE WORD *feedback* bother you? Are you weary of jargon from the social sciences and engineering creeping into your artistry? Well, hang on. The concept is vital to your ability to improve. It is only through the constant, unspoken use of feedback that reporters like Ms. Turner seem to effortlessly crank out superb leads. They have constructed a mental loop that forces every key thought to be tested—to be fed back for analysis—before it is put on paper.

Next time you're in a newsroom and you hear a reporter whining for the tenth time in an hour and a half about his "writer's block," remember what's probably happening inside him. It's not that the words won't come; his mind is producing plenty of combinations of words. The problem is that each new combination of words that his mind produces is being tested against his lead filter—and is promptly dashed against the rocks. It's not that nothing's coming, it's that nothing works.

And so it is with Ms. Turner. Do you know the feeling of simply typing out whatever comes to mind? Of letting the wave of words spill out and crash against the paper? Turner doesn't. She is one of the most calculating people you have ever met. Before any thought is turned into a typing impulse, it is double-checked. Diagram 3.1 illustrates the process. The style of simply letting the words flow out, on the other hand, would look like Diagram 3.2. See? In the latter example, there is no quality control.

If the reporter who just "lets it flow" were a machine, he'd be an electric fan, blowing his energy into space. If you played the same analogy game with Ms. Turner, she'd be an air conditioning system, constantly monitoring the temperature, feeding back the information to a central control mechanism, which then adjusts the room temperature to the system's goal—say, 72 degrees.

Take a second and pick up something, such as a magazine. As you move, your brain is sending motor impulses to contract the proper muscles. As your muscles contract, sense organs send feedback impulses (via the sensory fibers) to your central nervous system,

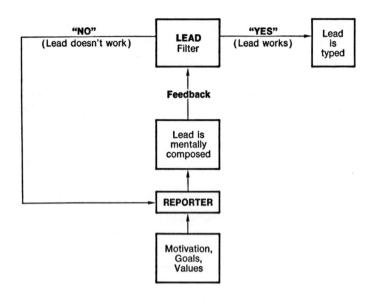

Diagram 3.1. *How feedback improves the lead.*

informing it of the degree of muscle action. Your brain responds by modulating or inhibiting further motor impulses until your hand closes around the magazine and lifts it. You take such a gesture for granted because you rarely fail at it, but in fact your system made constant checks each tiny step of the way. It measured each step against the goal of picking up the magazine; it closed the gap between the current state and the desired performance.

As we've seen, Ms. Turner's writing process works the same way.

It works because she is conscious of the need to make choices. Yet it is not merely the choices that make

Turner's work great, but the *way* she makes them. And it is here that most of us, in our formal education as reporters and writers, have been led astray. We have been trained to be average. We have been trained to think that we can match certain types of writing with certain circumstances. We have been given the impression that we can work through formulas. We have been told to sit down with books containing great newspaper lead paragraphs and analyze the styles, and then we have been lectured about the kinds of circumstances we'll probably face on the job, and how we'll mesh style with situation.

PRESTO! THE CREATION OF a crude thought process. Most of the time in the news business it will

Diagram 3.2. A weaker process–there's no feedback.

work; the reporter will make the right choice. But what happens when events start occurring in ways that defy the probabilities he has memorized? What does he fall back on?

His butt, that's what. He's in no position to judge the story on its own merits because he has been conditioned to see "types" of stories, and react: a narrative lead for one set of circumstances, a quote lead for another, an extremely terse lead for a third, a question-and-answer-type lead for a fourth.

Very, very crude. And that's what's behind so many editors' frustrations with reporters who can't seem to hit the mark when they tackle a difficult story.

Listen. Nobody can teach you how to write by simply showing you how words interact. It doesn't mean anything unless you can grab the reporter who wrote the words and ask, "Why? How did you make your choices?" You have to understand how his *thoughts* interacted to produce those words. You have to look at the causes, not merely the effects.

You can skim over a thousand examples of good leads and bad ones, and you can know the components of each, but that doesn't build your ability to make tough choices. It doesn't prepare you for the future. If anything, it produces a false sense of assurance that circumstances will fall into place, and that a certain type of lead will work. Sorry. Those styles of leads that look good now will develop weak spots when you apply them to tomorrow's news—new events, new components, new choices.

YOU CANNOT CONTROL THE NEWS, so you must compensate by developing sophisticated techniques to control the way you process it. Turner's ability to understand structure is the main plank, but there are two other peripheral considerations that go into each lead.

The first is a sense of values. You must instinctively pose a series of questions before you start composing: What is the purpose of this story? Who is it aimed at? What am I trying to accomplish? Hardest of all, you have to mean it.

Good writers don't have to consciously ask these questions; they flash on as part of the normal work orientation, the way the feeling of settling yourself in your chair tells you you're ready to begin typing. There are tough side questions, too: Do I need to make one last phone call? (After all, it's nearly midnight. . . .) Do I need to check the library again? (I've already checked it three times on this story. . . .) Should I go to that meeting? (It's important, but it's on a Sunday. . . .)

If you aren't asking yourself those kinds of questions before you start composing, start asking them. If you haven't built up the professional values that make those kinds of questions important, start planning another career.

The final consideration in writing the right kind of leads is a sense of exploitation. True, the word has an unpleasant connotation, but let it be. The hard truth is that in order to compensate for all the pressures against good writing in the news business, you have to push the facts as far as you can without violating the essence of the story or your own ethics. You have to develop the ability to squeeze out the juiciest, most interesting material. You have to be ready to pounce.

You may not want to admit this to many people outside the news business, but it's a fact of life. Look what your writing is up against—the pressure of deadline; the pressure of mediocre editors who don't understand the craft of writing and fall back on clever phrases like "Just tell the story"; the pressure to play it safe; the pressure to be average.

These institutionalized pressures push down on you; they conspire to flatten your writing, to produce the sameness that marks most news stories. You have to push up—fight against the pressure, overcompensate. Usually, you'll have to do so on your own, because once an editor on deadline judges a story to be accurate and functional, he'll usually buy it and begin editing it for grammar and interior phrasing. He rarely possesses the time or patience to consider restructuring it.

For an example, let's recall that plane crash story you worked on in Chapter 1, where you were trying to track down the pilot's address. It's now the day after, and you've come back to the newsroom after interviewing a passenger who survived. The city desk wants a second-day color story; it will run as a sidebar to the main piece about the cause of the crash.

An hour later, you hand in your story. The city editor begins skimming it:

```
    The chilling events of Monday's
Continental Airlines DC-10 crash at Los
Angeles International Airport are still
starkly vivid in the mind of John
Simmons.
        Simmons, 58, was aboard the 9:23
```

a.m. flight bound for Honolulu, Hawaii.
He sat in his living room today and re-
counted in a calm, steady voice the details of the crash that killed two persons and injured 74 others, but left him
unharmed.

"I had an aisle seat on the right-
hand side of the plane, near the front,"
he said. "I remember an escape hatch 12
or 15 feet in front of me.

"I felt the first tire blow. It
felt just like a blowout on a car. Then,
I guess the pilot applied his brakes.
You know, that puts a tremendous amount
of pressure on the other tires. I'm
sure I heard at least three more tires
blow."

AT THIS POINT THE CITY EDITOR ought to look up, open his mouth and bite your head off. How in the world could you fail to exploit a quote as juicy as "It felt just like a blowout on a car"?

What a striking conflict between a man's impressions and reality. A superb contrast: a shocking disaster that at first felt like an everyday mishap. How often do you find a follow-up angle that good? When they happen, you have to exploit them—you have to *stomp* on them. For goodness' sake, you can sacrifice the date, make of airplane and location from your first paragraph; anybody who read the paper yesterday—the day the story broke—already knows that. Your strategy today is almost mathematical: your ability to play with the structure of a lead is directly proportional to your audience's familiarity with the circumstances.

You would never have written that average lead if you had set specific goals for the story, based on what your audience knew and what you wanted to achieve, and if you had been conscious of the need to exploit your best material.

Ideally, your city editor understands these principles. And after he chews you out, he takes the time to type out the lead combination that screamed to be written:

```
     "It felt just like a blowout on a
car," John Simmons said.
     It wound up feeling far more explo-
sive.
     For Simmons, 58, a survivor in yes-
terday's Continental Airlines DC-10
crash at Los Angeles International Air-
port, the scene remained starkly vivid
today.
     "I felt the first tire blow," he
said.  "Then I guess the pilot applied
his brakes....
```

But you can rarely depend on your editors to improve a story like that; you have to take the responsibility. Your success in print depends upon how well you use your filters.

Now that you are conscious of developing a filter for

your leads, we must turn to a broader problem: developing the overall sequence of the story. As we noted earlier in this chapter, leads and sequencing are intertwined. Both processes involve the ability to shuffle and sacrifice elements, to set a goal and to focus on it. Neither process can be easily taught, because each is based on a reporter's willingness to push himself, to tell himself flatly, "That's not good enough"—even when he wishes desperately that it were.

4.

Sequencing

Within the unconscious, an automatic combining and recombining takes place until certain combinations having a peculiar affinity for our emotional consciousness occur, and bring themselves to our attention.

—Jules Henri Poincaré, nineteenth-century French mathematician

Everything is connected.

—A subject in a recent Chicago experiment in biophysics, describing her feelings during a "felt shift," a period of mental insight believed to represent higher-level reorganization in the brain.

ALL NEWSWRITERS, NO MATTER WHAT their deficiencies, can empathize with the words of both the "felt shift" subject and Poincaré. Everyone, at least occasionally, has had that feeling of his story suddenly falling together, each paragraph tumbling into place. Like the other skills we've discussed, it isn't magic; the best reporters take certain steps to achieve this organization.

Let's pick up where we left off in Chapter 3. The lead has been transferred from your head to the typewriter. Now what? You're pausing, and the pause begins to grow uncomfortably long. Unconsciously, you may be hoping to become caught up in a process described by B.F. Skinner, a controversial American experimental psychologist who explains all human behavior in terms of stimulus, response and reward for success.

"As we write a paragraph," he says, "we create an elaborate chain of verbal stimuli which alter the probabilities of other words to follow."

All newswriters have experienced this phenomenon. We count on the lead to spark mysterious rhythms that will propel the rest of the story, bringing forth the paragraphs in the right order.

And like all long-shot bets, it sometimes works. Writing the story one thought after another, seemingly without overview or preparation, is not impossible. But remember: When the technique doesn't work, you tend to look like an idiot in the eyes of your editor and readers.

A GOOD REPORTER OFTEN FOOLS his colleagues and himself by saying that he's banging out a story without formally organizing it, when in fact he has subconsciously put the story through a sophisticated set of organizational filters.

That's what we're looking at in this chapter: the most crucial component of solid news or feature reporting—sequencing. The best reporters master it by increasing their ability to hold a complete story outline in their immediate memory. They operate on two levels simultaneously, writing each paragraph with regard to its interior structure and its role in the story as a whole. They utilize written outlines, certainly, but the initial work—the mental spadework—is what produces the brilliance.

It is achieved by continuing the process we discussed earlier. The prime facts in the story have already been crudely sorted while the reporter gathered information, and they were roughly reviewed again when he wrote his lead. Now the process of putting the information in order must become more delicate. The facts must be viewed for their relationship to one another. The chronology in which the reporter collected the information must sometimes be discarded, and replaced by an outline of facts that emphasizes the essence of the story rather than the order in which events happened.

With that mental outline prepared, the reporter begins typing, pausing for countless brief interludes in which he scans that outline to make sure the paragraphs are being ordered correctly. So highly tuned is this skill that some reporters insist they bring up each paragraph from a deep, dark well that they do not understand. These are the people who cruise through a sparkling five-take story in the last forty-five minutes of deadline and confound you later in the day by saying, "Man, it was flowing good this morning."

Obviously, the inborn quality of that reporter's mind has something to do with his ability to hold a great deal of organized data in mental limbo for instant recall. But God-given ability is only part of the story; the newspaper world is filled with reporters who don't pay regard to the development of this skill, who don't try to incorporate it, who too often work from paragraph to paragraph, waiting for that infrequent sensation of the story falling together. It doesn't come unless you concentrate, and the reporters who don't concentrate on improving their sequencing abilities are often the ones who receive the most elementary assignments: their editors grow convinced that they simply don't have the brains to handle complex stories.

To improve you must first consider the mental attitudes that produce good sequencing, and then apply them throughout each coverage situation—not merely when you sit down at the typewriter.

Sequencing is a mental act that follows a natural process in the brain which psychologists call *integration*—recognizing that various parts would form a unified pattern if they were all shown together.

For example, when you look at a truck, you don't see all the relevant details at a single glance. Your eyes rove over it, observing first one part, then another. Your total perception is not the same as the result of any one glance, but rather a product built by integrating the data from many different glances. If your visual system is working properly, you see that the trailer is linked by a heavy metal brace to the cab; if there's something wrong with your system, perhaps you see two separate vehicles. Similarly, if your sequencing system is working, you will be able to combine two seemingly disparate comments that were made a half hour apart in a press conference; your sense of overview will find that they belong together. If your sequencing skills aren't developed highly enough, you'll miss the connection.

SEQUENCING IS NOT MERELY a two-gear process, in which overview and immediacy must mesh. There are in fact a number of mental attitudes—a number of mini-filters—operating at once. They put simultaneous pressure on you to organize your story with respect to various newswriting values. The skilled reporter stands out because he has learned to instinctively balance these attitudes, so that each provides the proper tug on his attention while he writes. Average reporters may be conscious of these tugs, but they respond more crudely, sometimes overcompensating and thus throwing their writing out of kilter. The reason there is no limit to the mastery of newsthinking is that there is no limit to the precision with which these sequencing attitudes can interact.

It's important to understand that no two reporters would use the same terms to define this balancing act. We all have trouble describing such delicate professional mechanisms. And we each tend to emphasize different natural processes in evaluating how well our writing systems are working at a given moment.

Some reporters—myself included—are most conscious of their kinetic systems (body motion) when they write. They measure their effectiveness by the way it "feels"—the rhythm, the subtle physical movements. It's a rather fuzzy standard, but the writer learns to trust it. As an example, I remember periods of remarkable speed, clarity and verbal unity at the typewriter during which I began feeling like Ray Charles at the piano—strong, distinctive rhythm, inexorable flow of words. For a while, that feeling became a standard, a level to compare myself with. But not all writers check their writing process that way. Some emphasize their audio systems, measuring their performance by the way the story sounds in their inner voice (see Chapter 8) or how the clicking of the keys sounds to their ear; others are most conscious of visualizing the words in their heads, and judge their effectiveness by the clarity with which that process takes place.

Listen as James Michener illustrates the diversity:

If I had a daughter or son determined to be a writer . . . naturally I'd expect them to be competent in their own language and to know something about psychology and the history of what fine writers have accomplished in the past. But the two courses I'd make obligatory would be one in ceramics, so that you could feel form emerging from inchoate clay. I think this is very important, that you have a feeling for form and a sense of how it's achieved.

And the second course would be eurhythmic dancing, so that you could feel within your own body the capacity that you have for movement and form and dramatic shifts in perspective. Of course, if you can't locate a class in such dancing, you might pick up the same sensations in a long game of basketball or tennis, where the ebb and flow of movement is pronounced. Or perhaps in any other sport requiring bold shifts of movement. What the artist requires is a sense of emerging form, a kinesthetic sense of what the human body is capable of. If you marry those sensory capabilities to a first-rate brain, you have a good chance of becoming an artist.

WITHIN ANY SYSTEM THAT A REPORTER uses to tell himself whether a story is flowing properly, there may be hundreds of individualized tricks or tip-offs. These differences are a major reason why it's pointless for anyone to offer the ultimate description of how good writing should "feel."

Nevertheless, one step is always there: the process of feeding back the chosen order of paragraphs through a "sequencing" filter. Every few paragraphs, the big question must be answered: Is the sequence working? The mechanism is similar to, though more complex than, the filter for leads that was analyzed in Chapter 3.

First, you choose the prime facts you feel are needed for the story; then you give each prime fact a code word—one short word that symbolizes the information—to make mental and handwritten outlining more streamlined; then you pick an order for the prime facts, trying to determine how many paragraphs will be required to develop each fact.

Now you begin typing, developing each fact—but before you get too far, stop. Feed your copy back through your mind's sequencing filter. Does the story represent the essence of what you know? Is it going in the right direction? If the answer is yes, keep typing. If it's no, start over—and don't just start rewriting, start *rethinking*. Put yourself through the entire sequencing process again, as illustrated in Diagram 4.1.

There is no systematic guide to constructing a process like this, but try to build your own feedback style—with your own rules and tests—until you eventually begin shaping sharp outlines subcon-

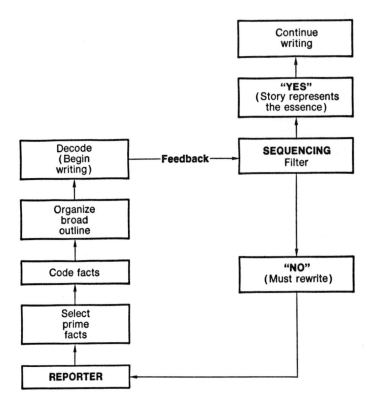

Diagram 4.1. The sequencing process. If the reporter does not combine the paragraphs properly, his filter instructs him to try a new sequence.

sciously. To get there, use these kinds of mental attitudes:

LOOK FOR THE PATTERN. If you built a proper framework to search for your facts and then diligently stored the facts in your mind, you're on your way. Still, you have to scan your prime and secondary facts again for relationships between them—connections that may have seemed unimportant when you were gathering the information.

DISCARD THE CHRONOLOGY. Human nature and the pressures of news work conspire to tilt reporters toward writing stories based on the order in which they witnessed events. Many times, that's the only way a particular kind of story can be written.

The more crucial times are those when an average story—structured upon the chronology the reporter witnessed—can be made great by decisively abandoning that order. You see examples of this restructuring all the time, but the effort it requires is often invisible; the better it's done, the easier it seems.

Example: You interview a county assessor who's under fire for unequal appraisal of property; then you interview three homeowners who want to recall him. Your story order runs something like this: a graph or two for the homeowners' general charges, then a graph or two for the assessor's response, then a list of specific charges, then a list of the assessor's specific responses.

That's average. Improving it is easy: Integrate the charges and responses so that each charge is immediately followed by the assessor's answer.

That's better, but the reporter who is willing to abandon the chronology in return for excellence can go even further—and in a completely fair manner. Remember the first sequencing attitude we mentioned: "Look for the pattern." If there are a dozen charges, see if they can be combined into four or five broader groups. Don't be satisfied with one alteration of the chronology; further modification is often essential in getting to the meat of a story.

Example: You've interviewed a filmmaker whose next movie is about the Turkish massacre of one and a half million Armenians in 1915, an incident the filmmaker witnessed as a small child. You could structure the story in two major halves—the filmmaker's experiences during the massacre, and the standard details about the film—or you could start carving up the chronology of your interview.

Here's one way. Start with three or four lead paragraphs that combine a summary of the historical event and the news that the film is being made. Then use a typographical transition device (extra white space below the last introductory graph, for example) and begin the narrative of the horrors the filmmaker saw as a boy. Exploit his quotes. Then use another transition device to break the chronology and come back to the present tense for some more information about the film—its cost, how it will be marketed, and so on.

The advantage: With the less adventurous approach—telling the story in two halves—the reader would have enjoyed only one counterpoint, the transition from film to real-life terror. With the more sophisticated approach, there is a second counterpoint, a second shift in the flow of the story. Now the reader understands both the terror in terms of the film and the film in terms of the terror. You have more deeply communicated the emotion of a man trying to portray his own horrors.

There are countless other techniques, but again, it's not this book's purpose to develop a catalog of styles. The *intent* is the key, and it is one of the most important lessons to learn: Don't be bound by the order in which events occur, unless that happens to be the best way to tell the story.

TRANSLATE THE ESSENCE. Parlay your skills. Your ability to see patterns and discard the chronology should have produced the insights that formed the roots of your story outline. From there, begin asking yourself some sharp questions. Precisely what is the *effect* of the merging of my facts? What does my story really *say*? Does my outline successfully translate what I *know* into the story? Does it communicate the *essence*, rather than just a handful of details?

When seeking the essence, the writer is prodded to go further than merely setting down one side of a story and then the other. He pushes himself to add perspective and depth to the structure of the report.

DEVELOP THE FEELING OF BEING READY to volcanically erupt. Try to gear yourself to react strongly when your mind reaches insights that strengthen the story outline. Have confidence that there is one "best" method of sequencing each story, and that you will recognize it when it suddenly appears from under the surface of your consciousness.

ISOLATE. To find that "best" outline, you have to narrow your focus. Decide which parts of the story are hardest to tell, and separate them from the remainder. The better you can isolate a problem, the more strongly your beam of concentration can tackle it. Ask yourself, What are the large problems in organizing this story? What are the small ones? What should I sacrifice? All problems have "fuzz" around them, which makes them appear large. Get rid of the fuzz and you'll become more aware of the core of the problem.

SCAN YOUR PRIME FACTS METHODICALLY before you begin to develop an outline. Break them down several ways. First, consider each prime fact; then create two piles of prime facts, the most usable in one, the rest in the other. Then sift through the most usable facts again, further limiting the number that are essential to the story. Again, develop your own organized process. Eliminate broad classes of data and then narrower ones, until the final set of facts—the set of facts you will use—has been separated from everything else.

THINK OF YOURSELF AS A PAINTER who instinctively strives for that fine line of balance between foreground drama and background detail. Unless you are conscious of attaining an artistic balance, you will fall into traps: lead paragraphs overloaded with detail; four-paragraph quotes that should have been cut down to two paragraphs; technical descriptions too high in the story, blocking the reader from continuing to follow the essence of your report.

DEVELOP A RHYTHM IN YOUR PHRASING. Try to blend long and short sentences and a variety of styles into this sequencing maneuver. Your mind should not be devoted solely to the ordering of facts when you build the outline; any offbeat phrasing techniques you may use will influence how well the sequence works.

LEARN TO SAY NO TO YOURSELF. Develop the discipline to separate your good impulses from your bad ones. Many "good" ideas simply don't work well in a news framework, or take exceptional talent to manipulate. Depend on your news values to warn you when a certain style of sequencing threatens to make the story misleading. You must be able to visualize the story as a whole, take a couple of steps back and ponder its overall impact.

The difficulty in making these sequencing attitudes work together may be compared to bowling. Imagine yourself on a lane in a bowling alley. As you make your approach and throw the ball, you are making several calculations at once—eyes, arms, legs, head each trying to combine with the actions of the others. People who bowl for fun have trouble improving their scores beyond a point because every time they adjust one part of their approach (such as the arm swing), it throws all the other components off. Professional bowlers are patient enough to tinker with each part of their game, making countless adjustments until each component is operating at ultimate effectiveness. Then they tinker some more to perfect the way each step blends with the others. Because they are human beings rather than machines, the best bowlers average only 200 to 220, rather than the perfect 300 score.

The mental attitudes that control sequencing must be properly coordinated in order to propel the facts (the bowling ball) down the lane to hit the reader (the pins) with maximum accuracy and impact.

MONITOR YOUR IMPROVEMENT in orchestrating the interplay among these attitudes. Be conscious of reaching a plateau, then leveling off, then climbing to a new, higher plateau, and so on. In working your way up to a new plateau, you will be slowly achieving the maximum development of one order of writing habits. Reaching the plateau means that that order has become sufficiently automatic for you to concentrate on a higher order of habits—the next plateau.

For example, consider a single sequencing attitude: the balancing of foreground and background information. For a month or two, a reporter who has not paid formal attention to this balance will have to prod himself to consider the relationship every time he writes a story. After a time, the balance factor will come to his mind automatically, and the calculation will be made seemingly by instinct. Now the reporter can use his energy to examine more sophisticated balance factors—for example, the relationship between information in the first two paragraphs, rather than the more crude balance between the two halves of the story.

Most skills in newsthinking seem to fall into this hierarchy of habits. When a reporter manages to sufficiently master a higher order of skill, the steps are "lost"—they remain, but they no longer must be taken consciously. They have been blended into his lower orders of habits, and serve as a foundation for progress to the next higher order. In the art of sequencing, that relationship explains why skilled reporters can produce a story without seeming to think about it. They have perfected even the highest-level writing habits, freeing themselves to focus most of their concentration on a relatively small number of sophisticated variables. A roster of difficult considerations can be resolved immediately: the story is outlined in depth; the outline has been shaped with attention to dozens of "outside" factors, such as the amount of space available, the deadline, the sensitivity of the copyeditor to whom the story will probably be routed, the other stories the paper has published on this subject in the last two weeks, the follow-up story it may publish tomorrow, the amount of attention competing papers have paid to this story—and unlimited additional considerations.

That's why a skilled reporter can be typing furiously with twenty-five pieces of notepaper strewn across his desk and a telephone clamped to his ear when he suddenly pauses, tells the caller to wait a minute and shouts a question across the city room: "Is Smith's story coming in today, or is it holding?"

Background: The reporter knows his story and reporter Smith's are the last two to be turned in before deadline. His caller has provided a piece of information that can be developed to quickly supplement today's story—but not without using another eight or nine paragraphs. Is Smith's story going in today? If so, there's probably not enough space to warrant the extra time our reporter needs; he'll be better off using the time he has to polish up the story as it's now written. He can go after the new item separately for tomorrow's paper. But if Smith got tied up, the situation changes; our reporter will tell an editor about the potential addition and see if the desk wants it for today's edition.

What is sophisticated here is not the judgment itself, but the ability to make it amid deadline chaos. The habit of checking such factors in similar situations has been learned well enough to be triggered without conscious attention. That may not be a habit vital to pure "writing," but its usefulness to newswriting is obvious.

Try, then, to reach plateaus in which you increase your ability to hold a broad outline in your head while playing those various sequencing attitudes against each other. Envision the small units that comprise your basic skills. Try to feel as though you are combining those units, so that they begin to happen in bursts of threes and fours—or tens and twenties—leaving you free to concentrate on bigger questions. Among the biggest: that quick, back-and-forth shift between the paragraph or sentence just coming onto the paper and The Big Picture—your mental overview that dictates how your paragraphs should be combined.

Now it's time to venture into more murky but equally vital territory: your memory, your most important tool in this delicate exploratory surgery of sequencing, and your most elusive ally in newsthinking.

5.

Memory

"The horror of that moment," the King went on, "I shall never, never, never forget!"

"You will, though," the Queen said, "if you don't make a memorandum of it."

—Lewis Carroll

THE MAYOR OF THE TOWN YOU COVER is about to appoint a new city commissioner. The choice is crucial because of the current political balance of the commission. Out of nowhere, this afternoon's edition of a competing newspaper breaks the story, revealing the mayor's appointment—hours before the ceremony in which the announcement was to be made.

As the city hall reporter, you had been trying to obtain the same story for your paper, but hadn't gotten anywhere and had resigned yourself to simply writing a story for tomorrow morning's edition based on tonight's formal announcement. And now you sit, teeth grinding, egg running down your face, holding a copy of the rival paper.

How did your opposite number get it? Luck? A tip? A good guess?

It began with mental skill—with another mental filter employed by your competitor. This one forced him to conscientiously run each new story through his memory.

Your rival beat you by exploiting his memory and his ability to see patterns. In groping for a way to elicit the name of the new commissioner, he remembered a similar incident in 1973, in which ABC television broke the news that President Nixon would appoint Representative Gerald Ford of Michigan as vice-president, replacing Spiro Agnew, who had resigned under allegations of corruption. A few hours before Nixon went before TV cameras to make his announcement at a White House ceremony, ABC learned that the entire Michigan congressional delegation had been placed on the White House invitation list. Reporter Bob Clark then confronted Ford with that information, and challenged Ford to deny that he was the vice-presidential nominee. Ford was forced to acknowledge it, and Clark quickly went on camera with the announcement, scooping the rest of the news media.

It made an impression on your opposite number. When the problem of finding out the identity of the new commissioner arose, the similarities between the two situations struck him. He went to work.

Fortunately for him, there was a city hall guest list being prepared for that night's announcement. And the list included several members of the neighborhood advisory council that was headed by the suspected appointee. From there, the reporter had it made.

HE HAD IT MADE BECAUSE he saw a pattern. Without that, he would have gotten the scoop only by pure luck—a friendly source tipping him off about the guest list, for example.

His success was another illustration of the importance of a sophisticated memory. An efficient scan of historical parallels gave him his hunch.

Similar memory links come into play throughout the newsthinking process, but for now concentrate on the effort you make to see patterns. This is a crucial stage, because it is one of the few variables that can be controlled (to a degree) in order to improve your use of memory.

Consider for a moment the standard conceptualization of the human information-processing system in Diagram 5.1.

Now, as you read the rest of this chapter, think about your own system, and how it functioned during the last story you worked on.

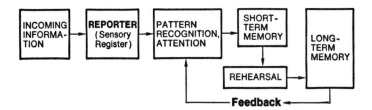

Diagram 5.1. The information-processing system.

EACH PIECE OF DATA YOU CONFRONT—a face on the street, the taste of a hamburger during lunch, a line of figures in a city budget, the annoying ache of an ingrown toenail, a newscast about a vice-presidential nominee—enters your system by one or more of your five senses, and is held briefly in sensory form.

The information remains in these "sensory registers" for only about a second, but while it is there two important processes take effect. One is pattern recognition—the ability to link the new information with previously acquired knowledge, coding it, giving it meaning. The other factor is the mind's state of attention—the degree to which it is "tuned in" to the incoming data. In other words, how hard you're concentrating.

Will the glob of type you're looking at or the noises you're hearing be given meaning? Will you interpret them as words, or will they fade out of your consciousness after a brief stop at the sensory register? Whether the information is routed to your short-term memory depends upon the degree to which your pattern recognition and attention skills are working.

Even if it gets to the short-term memory, the

information will disappear quickly unless you keep it alive by "rehearsing" it—repeating it several times, either out loud or to yourself. If that is done, the information will probably be filtered into the long-term memory, where the capacity is virtually unlimited. There are only guesses about the amount of information held in the average long-term memory; researchers have estimated anywhere from one and a half million to a billion trillion (12 to the 21st power) "bits."

HOW DOES THIS ALL HAPPEN? And how do you improve it? That, as we mentioned at the end of the chapter on sequencing, is where the murk begins.

A psychologist can tell you how your memory contributes to your mental processes, but if you want to go deeper and ask a neurologist precisely how the nerve cells in the brain organize memory, he'll probably scratch his head. An old consensus—that memory occurred in a specific area of the brain—died because no scientist was ever able to find the area.

Today, a variety of brain theories compete. One explains your memory by analogy to the *hologram*, the most sophisticated principle of information storage yet known. In essence, it reasons that the brain has a system of connections that are formed by paths traversed by light; this system supplements the brain's well-known system of neuronal pathways.

In a hologram, information is recorded on a photographic plate. The hologram can be cut into smaller and smaller pieces without destroying the stored image—the message is repeated tens of thousands of times. In a similar way, this theory holds, memory is scattered throughout the brain, upon the light paths, not unlike waves from a pebble tossed into a pond. When we remember something, we are engaging in reconstructive thought—sort of assembling the dismembered hologram.

Less complex analogies abound. We hear the memory system compared to the circuitry of a computer, an elaborate cross-filing system, an inexorable scanning device. One ten-year study by Bell Labs found that the human brain sweeps through its entire repertoire of relevant data even *after* it has found an answer to a question. Its speed: about thirty items a second.

The power appears awesome, and if we cannot expect to know where it comes from, we can at least provide some insights into how memory skills influence your work, and about how you in turn can exploit your memory by understanding its potential and its limitations.

Memory is what allows you to utilize a system of newswriting values. Without it, a reporter could not remember to process a story through a constant system of mental filters; each assignment would be a scattershot affair.

In turn, your memory system is stimulated by the use of an organized series of filters. Consider the chapter on sequencing. The reporter's memory brings each of the many sequencing attitudes into play as the story is organized; from this confluence, new thoughts begin to flow—thoughts unleashed by the meshing of old memories (the standards on which the filters are based) and new patterns (the story at hand).

MUCH OF THE BRILLIANCE you find in an outstanding news story can be attributed to memory. The story's perspective or interpretation is usually sparked by a flash of thought that makes sense of new developments by comparing them to previous ones.

The best reporters understand the importance of this sometimes mystical instant—when a thought or event is recalled and makes everything else fall into place—and they work hard to encourage it. They know when to prod their memories, when to hold an idea suspended while they search for parallels, when to fish back in their minds for additional situations—in short, when to push their memory systems. And, just as important, when not to.

As in sequencing, natural ability must be considered in evaluating your memory. Take this example: You're trying to decide in which order to deal with your prime story facts, and you've instinctively coded each fact into a key word so it's easier to organize them in your mind. But you have eight facts to deal with, and you just can't seem to juggle that many in your head at one time. You keep getting lost.

Why? Probably because you have an average mind. According to psychological studies, there is a tight limit on the number of bits of information that can be held at any one time in your short-term memory. The average is seven, with a range of five to nine bits.

Thus a reporter with a superior mind could keep those eight story facts flowing through his short-term memory, remembering them all while he arranged them in various combinations. The same mind could probably also adjust with relative ease to a system of eight-digit telephone numbers. Many of us, meanwhile, would find ourselves having to write down more new phone numbers in such a system, rather than temporarily holding the information in our short-term memories and rehearsing it as we dialed. Without rehearsal, information in the short-term memory will decay and disappear in about fifteen seconds. With sufficient rehearsal—sufficient quick use—the information will usually be transferred to the long-term memory, which holds everything from your birthday to your aunt's maiden name.

TAKE ANOTHER GLANCE at Diagram 5.1. Among other things, it illustrates the reciprocal agreement between your long-term memory and your mind's "pattern recognition" facilities. The "feedback" arrow, which plays a critical role in information gathering and newswriting, is also the mechanism that allows you to pay more attention to a face you recognize than to a stranger's. And while that process occurs unconsciously scores of times a day in everyday life, it is also responsible for triggering most investigative reporting. It is responsible for many of the brightest follow-up questions posed in press conferences or interviews. It lies behind much of the cleverness in an eye-catching feature story. It was what led to our hypothetical newsbreak at the beginning of this chapter.

Using their inmaginations in unpredictable ways, the best reporters have devised complex, individually tailored strategies to exploit their memories. They have become experts at organizing large chunks of information by cleverly coding and combining them, compressing the data until it can be squeezed into the capacity of their short-term memories. And they have refined the process of rehearsal to keep that collection of coded elements recycling for unlimited new combinations of sequences.

Like a sharp professional gambler, these reporters sense which variables in their memory systems are the best bets—which ones can be controlled to the greatest degree. Over your next few assignments, give your own techniques some inspection.

Example: During an interview, do you feel forced to keep taking notes or free to stop at a particular moment to concentrate on *how* your subject is talking? Do you trust your memory to later recall the broad significance of what he's saying?

It's the same question we confronted in a more general way in Chapter 2: How do you divide your attention in a coverage situation? One quick answer is to use a tape recorder, but that doesn't solve the problem. Anytime you're covering a story, your mind still has several other directions to go at a given moment. Does it anticipate the next development? Does it analyze the answer it just heard? Does it place the last half-dozen answers in perspective? Does it concentrate on the reaction of other people? All this can't happen simultaneously; you have to choose.

Grow to appreciate the peculiarities and vulnerabilities of your own memory and you will be able to make better choices about what mental chore to tackle first. You'll know how much attention to pay to the question that pops into your mind, because you'll know how likely you are to forget it; you'll develop the ability to know precisely how long you can listen to a speaker before it becomes necessary to take a note; and you'll refine a parallel ability, a notetaking system tailored to the eccentricities of your memory, giving you maximum information in a minimal number of words.

When it's time to call on your memory, put these kinds of attitudes to work:

VISUALIZE. Professional memory trainers stress this technique above all others, and most reporters already employ it to some degree. It makes up for a surprising number of deficiencies in intelligence, motivation and concentration. By visualizing the facts you want to remember—coding them into images, pictures—you create stronger associative links in your memory system.

For example, if you're trying to remember a politician's theme of a balanced budget with a $200,000 surplus, create a picture in your mind—turn an abstract concept into a symbol. Picture a budget book resting on a balanced scale, with the scale reading "$200,000."

Or suppose somebody tells you that the smog level is .21 parts of ozone per million particles of air. Try picturing a 21-year-old researcher holding a measuring stick with an O-shaped bubble at the top of the stick, or a person of any age holding a stick that is 21 inches tall.

These kinds of tricks work because a word or number by itself doesn't mean anything to your mind; a symbol lends it meaning.

Try it with phone numbers. Suppose you hear 457-3522 and don't have a pencil handy. Create a picture. Envision, say, four 57-year-old men who are delighted to have just met a pair of younger women, aged 35 and 22.

ENVISION YOUR MEMORY AT WORK. Try to develop a mental model about how your own mind stores and retrieves information when your newswriting process is operating at its peak. That gives you a standard—a vague but important feeling—to aim for, to test yourself against.

Take one last glance at Diagram 5.1, the rough model of human information processing. Think about a recent assignment in which your memory contributed to the quality of a story. How did it *feel* to find information bursting to the surface of your mind with such crispness and decisiveness? How do you picture your mind *doing* it? How can you make it work that way again?

Sure, it's a game, but try it. Remember two weeks ago? You were working on a story about the extensive use of unicycles by a local physical education teacher. During the interview he used the phrase "helping movement-deprived kids."

Your mind responded. Somehow, that phrase sounded familiar, but you didn't know why. So you began systematically scanning your long-term memory, searching for a category of information that seemed to be connected to the new phrase. Eventually, you decided to mentally examine the science-related stories you had written recently. You narrowed that down to a series you had written on eye care. You narrowed that, in turn, to a small segment of the series dealing with physical activity in the visual development of youngsters. Finally, you zeroed in on one paragraph dealing with optometrists' fears about the influence of television.

The entire search gave you a chance to add important perspective to your unicycle story. In it, you noted that optometrists were warning that too much TV-watching and home video games were causing children to develop only a one-dimensional visual system, robbing them of the physical activity needed to learn how to "move in space."

That put the PE teacher's comment about helping "movement-deprived kids" into perspective. But not without a lot of mental effort on your part. You were ready to respond to a hint of memory; you concentrated; and you scanned again and again, sifting through narrower and narrower classes.

That kind of performance may well have been your optimum level. What kind of effort did it take to reach it? What will it take to do it again?

BE READY TO FIRE. Be ready to respond. Try to develop a feeling of an alert long-term memory that will eagerly flash on whenever it senses even a hint of a connection between new information and past experiences. At the same time, subject any patterns you find to rigorous criticism; don't fall prey to a hyperactive memory system that jumps to conclusions.

CONCENTRATE. Remember that the higher your level of attention, the more willing your mind will be to route new information to its storage banks. Don't presume that your powers of memorization are constant; if you read a document sloppily, you'll be able to recall a smaller amount of it. In addition, the memory links forged by that sloppy reading may be highly inaccurate.

Remember that everyone's memory has weak spots. Psychological studies of individuals who witness live events have shown a frightening amount of inaccuracy.

One experiment, conducted in a classroom several years ago, involved a staged attack on a professor in front of 141 persons. It was videotaped for comparison with eyewitness reports.

After the "attack," each observer gave a sworn statement describing what he or she saw. Most of them flopped.

For example, they tended to severely overestimate the time the attack took. They estimated the attacker's weight too high; they estimated his age too low. And seven weeks later, when each witness was presented with photographs of six suspects, only 40 percent identified the attacker correctly.

Twenty-five percent of the witnesses—including the professor who was the victim—picked as the culprit an innocent man who happened to be at the scene of the incident.

PRESS IT. Put your memory through scan after scan if the first attempt at retrieving information is not successful. Be patient. Try to convince yourself that the needed information is flickering somewhere in your brain's nerve cells, available—if only you can dredge it up. To motivate yourself, think back to the last time you *didn't* push your memory hard enough. You were searching for a thought that would provide an extra paragraph or two to flesh out a story, or give you enough of a hunch to dig up a related chunk from the library. You gave up, turned in the story, and the next day, for no apparent reason—aaarrgh!—the memory surfaced. It *was* there.

AND NOW, A FEW WORDS about forgetting . . .

> Memory—that strange deceiver!
> Who can trust her? How to believe her—
> While she hoards with equal care
> The poor and trivial, rich and rare;
> Yet flings away, as wantonly,
> Grave facts and loveliest fantasy?
> —Walter de la Mare,
> English poet and novelist

In 1930, a man named John McGeoch at the University of Iowa came up with a delightful little theory that there is no such thing as forgetting. Failure to remember, he explained, was actually only the failure to remember the right thing. The forgetter had simply not done a proper job searching the files of his memory.

Modern psychology, however, says no, thank you, to Mr. McGeoch, and uses *interference theory* to explain Mr. de la Mare's frustration over memory's capricious handling of grave facts.

It's a simple premise: If you are a librarian with a shelf of only ten books, you'll have little difficulty locating the proper one for a patron. But when the collection grows to a hundred or a thousand, it's no longer simple. More books are competing for your memory's direct attention.

Interference is any competing information learned either before or after a particular experience which prevents that experience from being properly stored in your long-term memory.

Example: Your newsroom is converting to video display terminals, and you're trying to learn the step-by-step procedure. But you keep mixing up the VDT manual with instructions from another computerized system you learned in another job two years before. That's *proactive* interference.

The other kind of interference—*retroactive*— includes any learning that occurs a few hours *after* you've memorized the new VDT manual, plus any other environmental distractions that might occur during that period. For example, the rock 'n' roll music that came blaring from the apartment across the hallway while you were studying the manual, and a series of chats you had a short while later after closing the manual in favor of that party across the hall. Because of the vulnerabilities of memory directly after learning, some specialists feel that the learning accomplished just prior to sleeping is the most effective.

TO SOME EXTENT, every perception becomes memory, but the long-term persistence of all perceptions would lead to an overflowing storehouse. It would be difficult to recall a needed memory at a future time. Much of what we view as our memory's flaws is explained by psychologists with the principle of *parsimony*—the memory's ability to operate with an eye to economy, retaining only what is needed.

You may, like Mr. de la Mare, cringe wistfully as you search your memory in vain for the wording of a lovely paragraph; but your memory has decided—for your own good—that you can get along with merely the recollection of the general sense of the wording.

Yet there are those who seem not to suffer at all from the slings and arrows of interference or parsimony—people who seem to remember everything. Their stories are almost completely pointless in the context of newswriting, but they are a tribute to human potential, and besides, they're fun to ponder. So relax for a few minutes and admire the skills of:

● Thomas Fuller, a black man born in 1710 and taken to Virginia as a slave. He could not read or write, but was able to perform astonishing feats of arithmetic in his head, such as multiplying two nineteen-digit numbers.

● Zera Colburn, born in Vermont in 1812, who began showing mental mathematics ability as early as age six. At eight, he toured England, where he performed before mathematicians and scientists and proved he could instantly multiply two four-digit numbers. Asked to raise 8 to the 16th power, he came up with 281,474,976,710,656 in a few seconds.

● Paul Charles Morphy, born in New Orleans in 1837, a world-famous chess player who often played championship games blindfolded. He claimed he could remember not only every move of the game at hand, but every move of every one of the hundreds of games he had played in championship matches.

● Johan Martin Zacharias Dase, a German who was regarded as a dull person—except when it came to math. He performed the most complicated problems that had ever been done mentally. Until his time, the record was the squaring of a thirty-nine-digit number; Dase multiplied two-hundred-digit numbers. As we have seen, the average person can hold no more than seven numbers in his short-term memory after taking a single glance; Dase could accurately count groups up to about thirty.

- George Parker Bidder, who, unlike most prodigies, retained his memory powers throughout his life. Born in England in 1806, he was being taken around the country on exhibitions by the time he was eight, and a few years later found himself pitted against young Zera Colburn in memory competition.

Bidder was thrown questions such as: A city is illuminated by 9,999 lamps, each burning a pint of oil every four hours; how many gallons are consumed in forty years? In eighty seconds, Bidder said 109,489,050 gallons.

But he apparently did not rely completely on numbers.

According to one story, a heckler once asked how many bull's tails would be needed to reach the distance to the moon. Unruffled, the boy answered that one would do . . . if it were long enough.

6.

Knowing the Reader

A FEW DAYS FROM NOW, when you're in the midst of typing, stop long enough to challenge yourself with this question: Why would anyone want to read that story you're writing?

Before you answer, consider the waggle dance of the honeybee. First decoded in 1945, the dance is one of the most complex of all animal communications systems. It goes like this:

When a foraging worker bee returns from the field after discovering a food source or desirable new nest site at some distance from the hive, it indicates the location of this target to its fellow workers by performing.

The pattern of the bee's movement is a figure 8, repeated over and over again amid crowds of other workers. The most distinctive and informative element of the dance is the "straight run" (the middle of the figure 8), which is given emphasis by the waggle, a rapid vibration of the body.

The complete shake of the body is performed thirteen to fifteen times per second, and at the same time the bee emits an audible buzzing sound by vibrating its wings.

The straight run represents a miniaturized version of the flight from the hive to the target. It points directly at the target if the bee is dancing outside the hive on a horizontal surface. If the bee is on a vertical surface inside the hive, the straight run points at the appropriate angle away from the vertical surface. Gravity and the position of the sun are used as orientation cues.

The straight run also provides information on the distance of the target from the hive, which is often accurate to within 20 percent of the correct distance, scientists say.

Now, the bee's techniques may seem to rival the more advanced properties of our language, but in fact they don't come close. We simply take too many of the complexities—and pitfalls—of the English language for granted, and therein lies the rationale for the next two mental filters we need to build: one that forces you to work with a sense of your audience, and another that forces you to inject perspective into your work. The latter will be covered in Chapter 7.

When you compare the waggle dance of the honeybee to the waggle dance of the human brain and tongue, the bee's version becomes a pretty simple affair. The straight run of the bee is, after all, merely an enactment of the flight the bees will take. The rules are always fixed, and the messages are always literal: they cannot be manipulated to provide new forms of information.

YOUR NEWSWRITING, ON THE OTHER HAND, is based on rules of linguistics which only the most advanced specialists care to fathom. Those rules—and those of our culture—provide us with a vastly larger array of messages than is provided by the mere presumed meanings of the words themselves. In addition, you can project an endless number of nonliteral images—fiction, lies, demagoguery—by the way you inform the listener or reader of your intent.

The possibilities are endless. Endless enough, certainly, to explain why so many newswriters get into trouble and can't provide their readers with a clear image. But by knowing your audience, you make the first move toward limiting the variables, toward isolating the target, toward narrowing the odds of miscommunicating. To the degree you are able to visualize your reader, you're developing another valuable test of what information to cut from your story, what to keep and how to sequence it.

You cannot succeed as a newswriter without developing this "readership" filter, this chore of perpetually asking yourself, "Who's reading this, and what does he know?" To ignore it is to proceed with an inflated idea of how a subscriber perceives your publication.

Don't kid yourself. No matter how important your newspaper or magazine or book is to you, it is no more than one of dozens of items on the periphery of the reader's consciousness. He rarely has the patience that many reporters' writing seems to demand.

It is not merely great writers who take pains to construct this filter; all great artists are aware of it. Listen to the late composer Richard Rodgers:

> All I really want to do is to provide a hard-working man in the blouse business with a method of expressing himself. If he likes a tune, he can whistle it, and it will make his life happier. . . .

Or actor and director Gene Wilder:

> I make movies for a fat lady in Kansas City. I imagine her weighing 280 pounds; I can picture her swatting flies on a hot summer's day and going to the movies every Friday night. And coming away saying, "Boy, did I have a good time. Did I laugh! Did I cry!"

ODD THINGS HAPPEN TO NEWS STORIES when the readership filter isn't used. For example:

• The afternoon paper, delivered to your door at 5 p.m., has a story about an event that "will occur at 11 a.m. today."

• Another story reports a price feud between the owner of the town's only trash dump and the local trash haulers, but never mentions the possible impact on the homeowner's trash bill. The reporter doesn't mention it because *he* knows that the city council, not the haulers, controls trash rates, and *he* knows that two weeks ago he stated in another story that the city wouldn't pass along the haulers' increased costs to consumers. Think the average reader knows or remembers that?

• A news report on a local planning agency's meeting is littered with technical expressions that are everyday lingo to the reporter and professional city planners—but not to the reader.

• In one story, the reporter has, somehow, left out the reactions of two key individuals involved. They weren't available for comment, but the reporter didn't mention that; he assumed that fact would be obvious by their absence from the story. The average reader, however, is just as likely to assume that the newspaper is holding back something—intentionally keeping part of the story hidden.

The readership filter works closely with the stance filter (Chapter 2), and these two filters often precede all others. The stance—that assortment of attitudes you employ to collect information—determines how you look for facts; knowing the reader helps you make better choices about how to use the facts you find.

In the same fashion as Rodgers and Wilder, you should play a psychological game with yourself. Obviously, there is no "average" subscriber, especially if you work for a paper that serves a sprawling metropolitan area. You have to use your imagination. You have to take stock of your paper's circulation and create your version of the fat lady in Kansas City. That doesn't mean you have to write your story in second person, or personalize every paragraph. It simply means you acknowledge that your first obligation is to your reader, not to your editors or to your sources. Pressure of deadlines and absence of sensitivity have eroded that truth in too many newsrooms, so that reporters write without an audience in mind. The nature of the craft leaves little time for questions like, "Why are we doing this?" A readership filter counteracts the pressure.

As we noted in Chapter 1, reporters of this generation are under a heavy burden to develop aggressive information-processing systems because of the huge increase in the amount of data that must be analyzed.

But it's not merely the growing complexity of the world that makes it harder to write; there's also the growing fragmentation of the American readership— your subscriber's increased willingness and ability to seek out specialized publications that appeal to his special interests. The more time he takes for them, the less time he'll spend with you.

The joint forces of a burgeoning "self-help" culture and a more economical printing technology have caused a surge of new magazines and newsletters to flood the country in recent years. Their focuses are narrow and precise: magazines for organic gardeners, for apartment residents, for owners of home computer systems; magazines for joggers, for riders of certain kinds of motorcycles, for divorced fathers who have custody of their children, for volleyball players—you name it.

This explosion of new, specialized magazines represents a direct challenge to that largest flagbearer of general circulation, the newspaper. While specialized publications can twist reality to meet the expectations and biases of their readers, newspapers have little such ability.

The competition extends to the individual reporter. Today, more than ever, he faces a heated battle for a subscriber's attention with each story he writes. He needs to use every bit of leverage available to him to make sure the subscriber will read not only the first two paragraphs, but the entire piece.

So work at it—try to figure how your product fits into the reader's world. Use your own knowledge of the political and economic makeup of your circulation area; consult your paper's market research department or government agencies; consider, too, precisely when your paper hits the subscriber's porch, and when and where competing media are delivered.

ONCE YOU HAVE ENVISIONED your typical subscriber, you can operate with more confidence. As you type the story, your phrasing will be more authoritative, crisper, because you'll be aiming it at a particular individual—not merely putting facts down on paper.

Employing the readership filter is frustrating not only because of the demands it makes, but also because sometimes you simply have to ignore it. Any sensitive reporter knows the feeling of being trapped, obligated by his news values to structure a story in a manner that challenges the reader. He knows the first two paragraphs will probably have to be read a second time in order for the average reader to grasp their complete meaning, but he also knows he has little choice: he just can't make the wording any more accessible without oversimplifying a crucial, complicated fact.

Even here, however, the use of the filter is beneficial; it provides something of an objective standard in a painful situation.

To put the filter into practice, here are some of the mental attitudes that should be developed and played off against each other. The reporter should pose them to himself as questions:

WHAT DOES THE READER BRING to the story? Remember that most good stories tend to be a series of progressions—over the course of several months, the story may require coverage a dozen times as each new development occurs. Keep in mind an idea of how much of your last story the reader can be expected to retain, and then take advantage of his background by systematically compressing old details.

In each new story, there should be a conscious shift of new elements upward and old ones downward. Segments that had to be explained at length in the first two or three stories should be drastically tightened and moved down. Prod yourself: essence, essence, essence.

Develop strategies—tricks—to accomplish this. One possibility is the use of code words in place of longer phrases or explanations that appeared in previous stories.

For example, when the news first broke, it was reported like this:

> County Assessor Jerome Pierce today was accused of deliberately underappraising a 100-acre parcel owned by the man who is managing his reelection campaign. . . .

Over the next two weeks, there were four follow-up stories in which the charges were gradually verified by the newspaper, so that by the fifth story the lead read:

> The Jerome Pierce appraisal scandal has convinced one-fourth of the county's voters to switch their votes and oppose Pierce's bid for reelection as assessor, a Daily Tribune poll shows. . . .

Without that sort of compression of old information, the new material would have to compete for the reader's attention. It should be given easier access.

Other considerations: Is your circulation area homogeneous in terms of income, race or sociopolitical attitudes? To the extent it is, you can make more valid assumptions—take more risks—about what your "average" reader knows; you can take more for granted. For example, if there is a high ratio of children to total population, you can develop a tendency to pump a little more detail into your education stories.

How many homes read both your publication and a competing newspaper? Let's say you work for an afternoon suburban daily of twenty thousand subscribers, and a morning metropolitan newspaper also circulates in your area. If the metro has five thousand subscribers in your area, you don't have to pay much attention to the way your paper handles stories that have appeared in the metro that morning; few of your subscribers will have seen it.

But suppose the metro has a local circulation equal to yours? You'll now want to be more conscious of putting "second day" leads on stories which, because of deadline differences, the metro carries first. You can't let pride affect your judgment; you have to acknowledge that a high percentage of residents probably subscribe to both papers. You have to offer your readers a later, follow-up version of the news.

Obvious? Sure, academically. But pick up the average p.m. paper and you'll see little difference between its packaging and that of a rival a.m. publication. Often it seems the p.m.'s editors are oblivious to the next question:

WHEN DOES THE READER READ IT? In a town whose work force is dominated by long-distance automobile commuters, the advantage of that a.m. paper is sharply stripped down. Many workers who take a morning paper may not have time to read it at length until the evening—they have to get on the freeway by 7 a.m. or so, and don't have more than a couple of moments over coffee.

Be honest about time differentials. Often you have to hedge your bet while writing a story. Example: An auto accident victim may be in critical condition at 11 a.m., but you can't report that he "is in critical condition today" if your paper isn't delivered to homes until 4 p.m. Suppose he dies at 2 p.m? " . . . *was* in critical condition *this morning*" is the phrasing that has to be used.

WHAT IS THE READER'S LEVEL of tolerance? In other words, based on the background he brings to the story, what do you have to *do* to make sure he reads it? How much luxury do you have in constructing your story? How many paragraphs can you take in getting to the essence? What do you have to do to hold the reader's interest once you get it? The variables are different in each story.

Often, however, the answer is mathematical. The smaller you feel the reader's interest in a story will be, the more careful you'll have to be to write tightly and cleanly—explaining the story's impact quickly to convince him to stay with you.

Conversely, if you have a story with obvious impact or interest—a 30 percent rise in the crime rate or a woman giving birth to sextuplets—you can relax a little.

WHAT QUESTIONS WILL EACH PARAGRAPH trigger? Here we're asking you to do the impossible: read your average subscriber's mind. Silly as it is, the effort will often avoid a problem we mentioned earlier in this chapter: the story in which the reporter's written logic leaps across several unwritten thoughts—the supporting facts, which the reporter took for granted, much to the dismay of the reader.

Those unintentional voids sometimes do more to

provoke disgust and distrust in a reader than anything else. Nobody wants to feel stupid; if a reader can't make sense out of your story, he's going to start reading something else—another story, or perhaps another publication. If it happens too many times, he's going to cancel his subscription; even in a one-newspaper city, there are a lot of other avenues for him to wander.

The readership filter and four other strategies to be described in the following chapters—providing the perspective paragraph, exploiting your inner voice, challenging your creative powers and editing your copy—are essential refinements that you must add to your bag of mental filters. They provide the polish needed for great writing. They are the filters that enhance the raw, mechanical talent for making the facts fall into place.

7.

The Perspective
Paragraph

WHAT'S WRONG WITH THIS STORY?

> SAN DIEGO—The man who became the first person to legally receive Laetrile imports in California is dead just short of his 75th birthday—a victim of the cancer he hoped the drug could halt.
>
> Ray Carnohan of Pacific Beach died of cancer of the pancreas late Saturday, three weeks after winning permission from a federal judge to bring the controversial apricot extract into the United States from Mexico.
>
> He is believed to be the first Californian to have been granted permission to import the substance.
>
> Carnohan, a furniture dealer, had told newsmen . . .

On and on the story goes, describing Carnohan's motivation for using the drug. Interesting piece, too, except for one chunk of information the reporter knew very well, yet didn't put in the story. It should have followed the second paragraph:

> Laetrile is banned by the federal Food and Drug Administration as ineffective in cancer treatment.

And with that lapse we embark on a little righteous indignation.

The night is dark and the moon is yellow and the leaves come tumbling down and a thousand dead editors break the silence, thrashing with frustration in their graves, still recalling all those otherwise bright reporters who never got the hang of that corny old command, "Tell the reader what it means." Reporters who never could seem to remember to insert that sentence about Laetrile's being illegal—that small fact that would have put the story in focus.

The dead editors howl in unison, demanding an answer for all the times they had to insert a "perspective paragraph" in an otherwise well-written story. Usually, it went just after the first, second or third paragraph. Usually, it was merely a dozen or so words that attempted to gently explain the significance of a story in terms of related events or opinions that had been voiced in the past.

They plead for an answer, these ghosts, but they'll have to be satisfied with this puny, painful-but-true conclusion: It's much, much easier to write a perspective paragraph than it is to *remember* to write one.

WE'VE REFLECTED SEVERAL TIMES so far on the number of forces and societal changes that buffet a reporter. To guard his sanity, he has to establish some frame of reference, some set of givens that hold true in the world. The trouble is, one reporter's given may well be a subscriber's key fact—a piece of information crucial to the reader's full appreciation of a story. The reporter, feeling the information is too obvious to mention, will leave it out.

Which explains why we have conversations like the one you're about to overhear, as the city editor reads the Laetrile death story in its original form, walks over to the reporter who wrote it and asks him to make the change we suggested:

CITY EDITOR: Say, Jim, you don't explain here specifically that Laetrile is illegal.

REPORTER (with a grimace; it is the third story he has knocked out today): Aw, everybody knows that.

Or: "Well, the story implies that much."
Or: "Well, hell, we can't spell out *everything*. We have to give the reader *some* credit."
The comebacks to those three answers: (1) No, everybody *doesn't* know that. (2) Implication is a game attorneys play. (3) Before we worry about giving the reader some credit, let's concentrate on giving him some help.
To the reporter who wrote the Laetrile story, the illegality of the drug had become a given. For a comparison, think about a citizen drafting a petition demanding clean air. Would he include information about how the nose inhales pollution from the atmosphere? In both cases, the writers try to avoid cluttering their stories with facts they consider obvious. In the reporter's case, that produced a mistake.

HOW CAN YOU PREVENT IT? By programming your reporter's mind to be conscious of the need for the perspective paragraph, a device that can lift many a story from average to good or from good to excellent.
The perspective graph (or graphs) is one of the clearest benefits gained from the use of the readership filter discussed in Chapter 6.
If you can make yourself conscious of writing for the reader, you are more likely to provide the perspective

that is necessary whenever you tell a story to another person—orally or on paper.

As you strengthen the hierarchy of newsthinking habits needed to build your readership filter, you will begin developing a more detailed cluster of skills— another mental filter—specifically tailored to the perspective paragraph.

This "perspective" filter will force you to automatically ask yourself two more questions each time you prepare a story: (1) Do I need a perspective paragraph and, if so, where should it go? (2) How should I word it?

From there, the sequencing and readership filters can be used to write and position the perspective graph.

Good newswriters don't just happen to trip over the element of perspective and luckily kick it into the right place in their stories. They are looking for it; they know its role and the punch it gives their work.

Unconsciously, they create the perspective filter, and every story passes through it. If you find yourself lacking that skill, start working on it. Write the word *perspective* on your arm with a felt-tip pen if you have to—anything to jab your memory. By the time the letters fade, the habit will have become ingrained.

What makes the perspective graph such an elusive little devil is the fact that it is often not conspicuous by its absence. A couple of examples from the spring of 1978:

• A wire service story reported that the FBI had informed two Nixon administration officials in 1971 that South Korean businessman Tongsun Park was making payments to U.S. congressmen under the direction of the South Korean government.

The lengthy story provided excellent detail about how Attorney General John Mitchell and Secretary of State Henry Kissinger were informed by the FBI. As a self-contained piece, it was good. What it didn't have, however, was a quick, direct reference to then-current investigations of the Korean payoffs, and a simple sentence stating that five years had passed between the time the Nixon administration was informed of the payoffs and the time the first public allegations of South Korean payoffs were made in 1976.

• A major California newspaper's veteran political reporter wrote an excellent analysis of the battle among Democratic and Republican gubernatorial candidates for endorsements from organized labor. As far as detail and an explanation of how the labor endorsement process is structured, the article was fine.

But it didn't address the question of what specific benefits candidates receive from a labor endorsement: additional volunteer workers, money, and the precious mention of the candidate's name in the newsletter that the union sends to each member prior to the election.

Obvious? Yes—to the reporter, the candidates he covers and most union members. But how about the rest of us readers? How about one sentence, three or four paragraphs from the top, beginning something like, "A major labor endorsement usually provides a candidate with . . . "

Hardly too much for a reader to ask, but of course most readers never get a chance to ask or to make suggestions. They must rely on how hard the reporter is willing to work to add an extra dimension to his stories.

Once your mind's perspective filter registers "yes," telling you there's a need, you can choose from among a number of methods of inserting the perspective graph. To show them, we will perform minor surgery on several stories that were published in daily newspapers. We'll separate the perspective graph from the rest of the story.

Our aim is not only to illustrate structure, but to emphasize how diligent you have to be. Most of these stories make perfect sense without the perspective graph. They did not scream for one; the reporters who wrote them had simply gotten into the habit of screaming "Perspective!" at themselves.

(The wording in some stories has been altered to change obscure geographic references, but the substance and structure are the same as they appeared in print.)

PERSPECTIVE WITHIN THE LEAD. On the left side of the page, we show the lead paragraphs minus the perspective material. On the right side is the original first paragraph as it appeared in print, containing the perspective.

NEW YORK—Voters Tuesday narrowly rejected Democrat Bella Abzug's bid to return to Congress and perhaps wrote a political obituary for the fiery feminist.

By just 588 votes, S. William Green, a Republican former federal housing official, was elected to Congress from Manhattan's 18th District, one of the wealthiest and most influential in the nation.

Lead that appeared

NEW YORK—In a surprising upset in a district with overwhelming Democratic registration, voters Tuesday narrowly rejected Bella Abzug's bid to return to Congress and perhaps wrote a political obituary for the fiery feminist.

WASHINGTON—The White House has virtually ruled out a swap of the best-known dissident now in Soviet jails, Anatoly Shcharansky, for one or more Communists in Western prisons.

That is the latest development arising out of secret communications regarding Shcharansky that reportedly have included veiled Soviet threats to "expose" more Central Intelligence Agency agents within the Moscow dissident community.

Lead that appeared

WASHINGTON—The White House, faced with stiff Soviet demands that could embarrass President Carter, has virtually ruled out a swap of the best-known dissident now in Soviet jails—Anatoly Shcharansky—for one or more Communists in Western prisons.

Orthopedic surgeons in Downey say they will stop taking new patients after Sunday.

The surgeons, who say they will not pay steeply increased malpractice insurance premiums which go into effect Jan. 1, say they will continue to treat patients they are caring for now.

It remains unclear how many orthopedic surgeons—as well as other doctors—in the Southland will continue to practice medicine after Dec. 31.

Lead that appeared

In the first joint action by doctors during the current medical malpractice insurance protest, orthopedic surgeons in Downey say they will stop taking new patients after Sunday.

PERSPECTIVE DIRECTLY AFTER THE LEAD.
This is the most common placement. It's for that reason
that our feedback diagram of mental filters (in the
Introduction) shows a story passing through the
perspective filter after the reporter prepares his lead
paragraph(s).

WASHINGTON—The Carter Administration Tuesday announced its long-expected decision to sell 50 fighter-bombers to Egypt in a Mideast package that includes some of the most sophisticated warplanes in the U.S. arsenal for Saudi Arabia and a sharply reduced supply of planes for Israel.

Some of the basic decisions in the $4.8 billion sale, which can be blocked by Congress, were made informally months ago, and were no surprise to close observers of U.S. Middle East policy.

Perspective graph

> It will be the first sale of U.S. warplanes to Egypt.

BOSTON—One of City Hall's lengthiest and stormiest battles ended Tuesday with Systems Development Corp. winning a $28.5 million contract to install a modern police emergency communications system.

The City Council voted 10-3 to award the contract to Systems Development. The losing competitor was the Motorola Corp.

Perspective graph

The decision ended 20 months of lobbying for the selection of a contractor.

LONDON — An influential Parliament committee Tuesday called on Britain's Labor government to make drastic cuts in immigration and tighten control of immigrants once they enter Britain.

The report, written by the House of Commons Select Committee on Race Relations, brought immediate protests from white liberals and immigrant groups.

The committee said Britain must not continue to allow the high level of non-white immigration of recent years.

Perspective graph

It seemed certain to fuel a growing political controversy over non-white immigration, which has stirred increased racial tension in this country.

WASHINGTON—President Carter's drive to win congressional repeal of the U.S. arms embargo against Turkey suffered a serious setback Thursday when the

Senate Foreign Relations Committee rejected the request 8 to 4.

By refusing to write language repealing the embargo into the fiscal 1979 military aid bill, the committee denied the Senate the opportunity for an automatic vote on the embargo when the aid legislation comes up for reconsideration.

Perspective graph

The committee's action means that the administration will now find it exceedingly difficult to get the full Senate to vote on ending the embargo, which the administration says threatens to weaken the North Atlantic Treaty Organization's southern flank.

DON'T BE AFRAID TO BREAK UP the essence of your story—the first two or three paragraphs—with the insertion of a perspective paragraph. If you have to sacrifice a little flow for a lot of interpretation, do it and don't sweat about it. That's a classic style-versus-substance confrontation, and substance usually deserves to win.

On the other hand, don't be surprised to find new factors that make it worthwhile to delay the perspective graph. Perhaps you have a particularly good quote that develops your story's essence, and the perspective paragraph you want to use is more obligatory than crucial. Here's a good example of the right choice of sequence in that case:

WASHINGTON—Publishing executives who had paid thousands of dollars for exclusive rights to H.R. Haldeman's memoirs reacted with consternation and bursts of anger after the Washington Post—which paid nothing—

—— **Essence**

scooped them all by running a lengthy account of the book Thursday.

"It's a shoddy way to do things," snapped Sidney Gruson, executive vice-president of the New York Times Co., which is publishing Haldeman's book, "The Ends of Power," Feb. 27 and had planned to begin running its own excerpts from the book Monday. "I'm not taken with this kind of journalistic enterprise." —— Quote

Publication of the Haldeman book had been considered important not only because he had been former President Richard M. Nixon's closest White House aide, but because he was expected to break his long self-imposed silence and criticize his onetime boss. —— Perspective

PLACING THE PERSPECTIVE five or six graphs down is often done in follow-up stories whose background is relatively well known. This technique was touched upon in Chapter 6: With each new progression in a developing story, move the old-but-vital information down and the new material up. Like this:

An initiative campaign aimed at putting a city employee "prevailing wage" issue before city voters in June has failed by a big margin.

That was the word Tuesday from City Clerk Rex Layton and City Councilman Ernani Bernardi, the leader of the campaign to put the issue on the primary election ballot.

Bernardi, while conceding that "apparently we have failed," said he would continue to work to get it on the ballot—if not this June, then next November or for the April 1979 election.

The councilman, in turn, was criticized by William R. Robertson, executive secretary of the county Federation of Labor.

Robertson accused Bernardi of waging "a campaign against city employees" that was financed by big business and kept moving with the aid of paid petition circulators. By contrast, Robertson told a news conference, Bernardi has been calling it a "people's campaign."

Perspective graph

The prevailing wage section of the city charter—for a long time one of the most controversial issues in City Hall—requires that the city pay municipal employees a wage at least equal to wages and salaries paid employees in the private sector for similar work.

Think about how many times you've seen a story like that made ponderous by the placement of the perspective paragraph directly after the lead. There's no reason for it. It's the kind of story which, judging from the version above, must have been in the news for months. You still need to explain this kind of story to those readers who haven't been exposed to it or have forgotten about it, but because of your previous coverage the number of such readers has dwindled; take advantage of that.

In newly breaking stories, however, feel free to string several perspective paragraphs together high up in the story. You're not blocking the reader from the news—you're merely reacting to the fact that sometimes it's harder to explain the significance of an event than the essence of it. Example:

Perspective graphs

An ordinance permitting the conversion of apartments to condominiums won unanimous but reluctant approval Tuesday night from City Council members.

Councilmen said they didn't like the idea of converting apartments to condominiums, but reasoned that the city staff now has some leverage it can use to discourage the practice.

The ordinance requires apartment owners to prove that at least half of the tenants in their buildings have "both a sufficient income and a disposition to purchase their apartment units as condominiums."

The action will be welcomed by some as a new inroad against the high cost of homebuying but criticized by others as a quick moneymaker for local apartment complex owners anxious to convert their units.

In actuality, it is neither. When council members last June put a moratorium on conversions, they also asked City Attorney James Longtin for an ordinance that would make such conversions almost impossible. That is just what they got.

It is unlikely that the council action will result in a wholesale conversion of apartments to condominiums. The new ordinance is more restrictive than permissive, which means conversions won't come easy. Apartment complex owners must do much more than simply decide to sell individual units as condominiums.

WHEN YOUR PERSPECTIVE FILTER tells you "no," remember the story about the golfing gorilla told in the introduction to this book: You do not hit every golf shot 280 yards down the fairway; sometimes you just tap it. Witness this:

> WASHINGTON—A secret six-year-old indictment accusing the brother of Panamanian leader Gen. Omar Torrijos of smuggling a huge shipment of heroin into the United States in 1971 was unsealed by the Justice Department Tuesday night.
>
> The indictment charged that Moises Torrijos, now Panama's ambassador to Spain, and four other persons smuggled 155 pounds of heroin aboard a Braniff Airlines flight from Panama to New York City on July 8, 1971 . . .

The story continued for several more paragraphs before the reporter mentioned parenthetically that the U.S. Senate was currently debating two treaties to end U.S. control of the Panama Canal. He then quickly returned to the details of the disclosure of the indictment.

Let's look at what the reporter did not do: He did not point out that news of the indictment of the brother of Panama's ruler might further cloud debate on the hotly disputed canal treaties.

In this case—on February 22, 1978—that perspective was sufficiently obvious to the average reader.

Controversy over the impact of the canal agreements had reached its peak; news coverage had been heavy. It was one of the relatively few situations in which the reporter could let inference do his work for him.

OVERREACTION. One example is all that is needed:

> WASHINGTON—A carefully orchestrated Carter Administration campaign to avoid a bruising confrontation with Congress over its controversial package sale of warplanes to Israel, Egypt and Saudi Arabia came under attack Wednesday on the eve of a key Senate test of the proposed sales.

First, let's analyze it by the numbers. Four descriptive phrases are used; two of them try to provide perspective, telling us about the attempt to avoid a confrontation and noting the tie-in with the upcoming Senate vote. It's just too much. Jupiter is less dense.

Is it readable? Yes, with a little effort. But is that kind of effort going to be worth the average reader's time? Is the perspective provided by each of those descriptive phrases really necessary in the first paragraph? Wouldn't the writer improve the story with a trade-off? If he could make the lead immediately intelligible to, say, 30 percent more subscribers by dropping two of the adjectives (using them in later references), wouldn't it be worth it?

Here's the most important question of all: Was the reporter who wrote that lead thinking about that balance, or was he overcome by the opportunity to cram all that perspective into the first graph, damn the readability and full speed ahead?

The ghosts of a thousand dead editors would appreciate an answer.

8.

Your Inner Voice

AND SO THE STORY IS BEING WRITTEN. The lead has been perfected, the sequence has been carved out. The other filters—memory, readership, perspective—have received the appropriate attention. The words can begin to flow.

But as they do, yet another important stage takes place, one that heavily influences the impact of the writer's words and his ability to string those words together in a variety of styles.

To illustrate it, let's revisit Ms. Turner, whom we last saw in Chapter 3 demonstrating the use of our lead filter. It's Monday morning in the newsroom and she's working, a bit leisurely, on a feature about an uneducated but well-read 84-year-old man who wrote a 400-year genealogical history of his family.

She writes, slowly, toying with the words:

```
When had the idea of chasing cen-
turies of his family's history popped
into the old man's head?  John Bowman
could only guess.  Twenty years ago,
perhaps, after he had retired; one of
his sons had given him what was supposed
to be a family crest.
     "That got me thinking," he said.
     He thought of the stories he could
tell--of sailing from St. Louis to India
in 1917 on an engineering job; marrying
the teenage daughter of an officer in
the British occupying force; returning
to America a decade later with a small
```

fortune, only to lose it in the Depres-
sion; and, finally, settling in Boston,
expanding the family and building a
business.

And there were the tantalizing
stories his father had told him--about a
Dutch mercenary who went to England to
fight for King Henry VIII; about the mercenary's grandson who sailed to America
as an indentured servant and changed his
name to Bowman, a tribute to the family's
tradition of skill with the bow and
arrow; and about the generations that
followed during the next 300 years.

John Bowman knew he was in the middle of all those stories, but he did not
know quite what to do with them. An in-
veterate collector, he had saved scores
of family documents, pictures and memories, but for decades their importance
merely germinated--until a year ago.

It was then, at the age of 83 and
with a fifth-grade education, that
Bowman began trying to sort out the family's legends and history.

The result was a surprisingly polished 122-page genealogical history...

Suddenly, there's a tap on her shoulder from the
paper's wire editor. There's a problem, a new

development in the Iranian hostage crisis, now in its seventh month. Two deskmen are on vacation, the editor explains, and since Turner isn't on deadline, could she come over to the wire desk and combine a half-dozen Associated Press and United Press International stories into one twenty-inch piece for the afternoon edition?

Ninety minutes later, the story is out of her typewriter. It begins:

```
In a coldblooded display of ven-
geance, Islamic leaders and other close
followers of the Ayatollah Ruhollah
Khomeini today displayed on television
pieces of the remains of the Americans
killed in Friday's mission aimed at
rescuing the U.S. hostages.
```

Remarkable. Compassionate, sensitive, measured phrasing one moment, and crisp urgency the next. Why, it's a marvel, to be able to switch styles of writing like that. Oh, to be blessed with such talent. . . .

AH, BUT BEING BLESSED WITH TALENT is hardly the complete explanation. Consider hard work. And imagination. And, finally, consider another mental filter, this one aimed at the delicate artistry of the inner voice—the strategies a writer uses to convert his or her thought impulses into words through silent speech. It seems to be a process all writers use, but with widely differing degrees of consciousness and risk.

Depending on the kind of writing you do, paying

increased attention to your inner voice can make you more aware of how you shape the wording of your story. With that awareness, you can try to exercise more control over the tone of the inner voice in order to increase the diversity of your writing approaches.

What Ms. Turner did was to abandon her everyday inner voice—the one she uses to talk to herself about such mundane matters as the grocery list—and consciously take inventory of the writing voices she has built up over the years. Did the story deserve a touch of awe? Lightheartedness? Sarcasm? Aggressiveness? Sometimes she can verbally describe the emotion or tone she is trying to inject; other times, she merely feels the urge to give the story a certain flavor—she can't say exactly what, but she knows the style she's searching for.

Finally, she made her choices. For the Bowman feature, she would compose in a leisurely, expansive voice, a voice suited to the sweeping nature of the man's accomplishment. He had sifted through history, and now so would she. For the Iran wire story rewrite, the choice was easier. She needed a voice of urgency, one that could tell a story with the proper mixture of terseness and drama dominated by the chronology of the event. A no-frills flight.

Through these maneuvers, Turner assumed her writing stance—a process similar to the prewriting, information-gathering stance we examined in Chapter 2. Here she created a filter to help deflect inappropriate impulses and prod her writing in the proper direction.

Once again, she was responding to the peculiar nature of the job of newspaper reporter—particularly the task of general-assignment reporter—and the flexibility it demands.

Look at it this way. If you're William F. Buckley, and your prime concern is a political column three or four times a week, your writing will be formed by a consistent inner voice; the column, after all, is intended to allow a writer with a relatively fixed point of view to interpret patterns of events. On general assignment it's almost completely reversed: you must cope with an unpredictable variety of assignments that require you to tell stories in any number of ways.

Thus it will not be merely the order in which you put your paragraphs together that determines how well you succeed; you must also be sure to select the tone of writing that best tells the story and best exploits its elements.

You do that through consciously adopting a particular tone of inner voice to compose the story—to translate your thoughts to the typewritten page.

Concentrate on this technique in order to take advantage of the power words seem to gain when the writer composes in a strong, confident inner voice and then transmits that force—as if it moved from his brain through his fingers—onto the page.

The more conscious you are of the technique, the more effective you will be in meeting the challenge of a story that calls for a precise style—sensitive, or bold, or urgent, or authoritative or any of a dozen others. Those kinds of qualities will help almost any story as long as the correct dosage is administered.

REMEMBER THE CONCEPT of "translation." It is a process a good newswriter engages in several times during the course of a story.

The initial stage, which we viewed in the sequencing process (Chapter 4), involves translating the chronology of events into an order based on the story's essence.

A second stage of translation occurs when the reporter reworks the technical or awkward phrases used by his sources (excluding quotations), putting the words into understandable English.

In both of these cases, a reporter can get away with far less than the maximum effort, and few editors will notice. It's the writer's intensity—his pride in craftsmanship—that determines whether and how thoroughly the translation will be made.

But regardless of how good a job he does in those first two stages, much of the work occurs mentally as the reporter outlines his story. Even if he makes the right organizational choices, he must continue to concentrate to insure their translation onto paper.

If he types too casually, believing the story will simply "flow," he may butcher the literacy and smooth sequence that he painstakingly created in his mental outline.

With this in mind, the skilled reporter learns to add an "inner voice" filter to his newswriting. He takes a moment to consider what kind of translation mechanism is needed to communicate the story, most of which still remains in his head. Before he begins composing, he poses the question, What kind of inner voice should I use to bring this story to life?

He has to make the right kind of choice; an inappropriate one can ruin a story, no matter how talented the writer is. If, for example, he adopts a slashing, staccato delivery for a soft feature piece about an eighty-three-year-old nun's last day teaching Catholic school, there may be no hope for him.

Some writers may quarrel with delving into specific styles of inner voice; they may feel it implies a coldly calculated approach to a skill which, after all, is considered an art—especially by people who are good at it.

And yet, if you follow a good newswriter's work over the months, you will be able to see that he intentionally changes his style depending on the type of story. The rhythms of sentence structure vary, the urgency of tone isn't always the same, the level of aggressiveness rises or falls.

The writer in question may not be aware—or may not admit—that he has built a repertoire of inner voices, but he has. He has also built a parallel skill that is just as important: the ability to match the correct inner voice to each story, or to invent new ones.

For example, if we press Ms. Turner about how she handled the Iran wire rewrite, we can drag this confession out of her:

"Well," she says, "I have this game I play with myself whenever I have to take a bunch of stories and compress them into a single wrap-up piece on deadline. I try to make it sound like [television anchorman] John Chancellor—I imagine that he's reading the final version on the air. First, I read through the material I have to work with, and then I compose in his voice. I'm trying to get the feeling of typing the words as though I were transcribing his version.

"Why does it work? I guess because I'm used to the rhythm of his writing—I watch his show a lot—and because his style *is* suited perfectly to that kind of job, where you have to make sense of a complex story within the limitations of TV airtime. He's great. That's why I steal from him, if you want to call it that."

My suggestion here is not that you concentrate on stealing other writers' styles, but that you take pains to first assert your own inner voice—a standard tone—and then develop a variety of supplementary voices.

WHEN AN EDITOR WORKS WITH A WRITER for a while, he grows familiar with the writer's inner voice(s), and begins to "hear" the story as he copyedits it. He becomes used to the better writers' ability to inject a great range of emotion, tone and pacing into their work. And he plods through the dullness of his less inspired reporters, who seem to write with few peaks or valleys in their construction.

But sometimes, to the editor's suprise, a reporter with a normally dull style produces an inspired piece. In the words of the delighted husband whose bumbling wife finally cooked a perfect medium-rare roast beef, what went wrong?

If you assume that the subject matter somehow lit a fire under the reporter, your assumption is too broad. A stage in between is the real key.

Yes, the subject *did* inspire the reporter—enough to finally make him *concentrate* on translating the force of what he felt to the typewritten page.

Countless other times, that reporter had been inspired by his material, but had not been able to *express* that inspiration. He had not concentrated hard enough on translating those perceptions, filtering them through his inner voice, and so when he composed his story the feelings weren't communicated.

A reporter more conscious of pulling those feelings out and putting them on the line would have done far better in similar circumstances.

And so I speak to the introverts in the audience: There are a lot of ways to enjoy a civilized life while keeping your feelings hidden—but not at the typewriter. You cannot wait for dramatic events to force you to express those feelings. That will improve your writing only in a smattering of cases. You have to *work* on bringing your thoughts out of your gut. The color, the sparkle, the liveliness that make good writing—they lie there.

We're not talking about altering the facts, or sacrificing basic objectivity. We're talking about the ability to write about a war-torn port, full of sunken ships and collapsed piers as "a smoking vision of hell." We're talking about a mobster's Cadillac that "gleamed like a huge blue steel egg." We're talking about being able to share our inner visions.

Let your inner voice be the spot where the icy orderliness of rationality and the uncontrollable blaze of emotion come together, shaping your composition.

CONSIDER A TYPICAL TEXTBOOK description of how thought impulses are crystallized into words. It roughly duplicates the process a reporter goes through in building his story framework and then his outline, narrowing his focus until he begins writing.

The first phase in this four-step thought-to-speech process is a state of awareness whose contents cannot be specified; at the most, we have only a vague outline of thought.

Then:

• The awareness qualities harden into crude ideas which form the general scheme of thought. Some animals may communicate when thought reaches this crude level, but we humans are more sophisticated; we do not yet speak. The thoughts are not sufficiently explicit to permit verbal expression.

• The scheme of thought activates a grammatical scheme; thought becomes further focused, until it is like the linear pattern into which the stones of a mosaic (the words) are to be fitted.

• In the final phase, we make the choice of the appropriate words—the filling in of the design.

Be conscious of the unity among those stages. When a good newswriter begins working on a story, he is launching a mental process aimed at forming a pattern into which words can be laid. Every step he takes determines how accurate the pattern will be; every step influences the next step. The scope of your research influences your ability to construct a good outline, and the strength and logic of that outline influence the ease with which you can translate your thoughts into a literate story. Each link in the chain of thought must be secure.

Then—and only then—can you flick a mental trigger and begin composing a story that meets your true potential. Give your inner voice weak material to work with and it will produce eloquent pap.

But give a well-planned, logical story outline to a surging inner voice and the magic begins to happen. The two forces build upon each other; the words are dazzling. This is the end of a long process of crystallization. A crude idea—a story angle—has been refined, time and again. Its words carry a power no one had anticipated, and when they reach the newspaper subscriber, they initiate another chain of energy. They begin making him think about the issue in question, setting off new ideas in his mind, until he begins a crystallizing process of his own, using the story to obtain a clearer perspective of his world.

Rarely are you lucky enough to see the steps merge, but you must believe they can. Whatever inner voice you choose to compose in, give it the spirit to transcend the moment; make it a voice that believes in what it is saying.

Conscious use of the inner voice can expand the writer's creativity. When he is pondering the phrasing of a story, he can try composing it in several different styles of inner voice, comparing the results in his mind.

Experimenting this way avoids the slight inhibition that crops up whenever a writer puts his impulses on paper. It's safer to do it in your mind, less embarrassing. (A good compromise is a VDT screen, because you can erase a bad start by pushing a button; there is no evidence to remind you of a failure.) The inner voice can run through a series of styles, and the reporter can listen. He can pick the approach and phrasing he wants, and then make the translation to paper.

As he does, yet another filter—the stuff of genius—comes into play. Let us pursue it.

9.

Tapping the Right Brain

The subjective must take back the world from the objective gorillas and guerrillas of the world . . .

—Lawrence Ferlinghetti,
San Francisco poet

IN THE NEXT TWO CHAPTERS we are going to look at your newswriting in the context of a commonly discussed creature called creativity and a little-understood neurological principle called "the right brain," the latter of which is one of the Next Big Things in progressive education and pop psychology.

Because your creative powers appear to be centered in the right side of your brain, we'll examine the brain issues in this chapter and discuss creative attitudes in Chapter 10. Together, the two chapters produce the background for the development of a "creativity" filter. Now let's get back to the newsroom, where we overhear a reporter making a common complaint to an editor.

The reporter is having a hard time doing justice to a potentially good feature story about a child stricken with leukemia holding on to life. When the boy was two, his parents were told he had six months to live. Now he is five—alive because of a series of surprising remissions. The parents are delighted and yet weary of the strain. The reporter, having interviewed them and the child, is weary, too.

" . . . and so what's happened is that I'm dried up," he tells his editor. "You had me working four straight months on that damn political coverage, and it soured me. All that structured stuff, I just don't feel like I can turn on my creative juices anymore—even with a piece like this one."

Most newspaper editors pride themselves on the ability to resolve a sensitive conflict like that with the reply, "Tough," or, "Just let the story tell itself." It's hard to blame them; there simply isn't time to sit down and say to the reporter:

"Look. Eastern cultures believe strongly in utilizing the subconscious, spiritual part of yourself to capture ideas that the day-to-day part of your mind omits or can't dig up. So I'd appreciate it if you'd concentrate on using that part—your subconscious, your subjective side—when you find yourself doing a feature or creative assignment."

Yet there is a compromise explanation—a way of looking at things—that any editor or reporter should consider when the creative fountain seems to run dry, when the writer needs to have faith in his ability to find a solution to a tough story.

It lies in understanding and then exploiting this scientific principle, refined only in recent years: A full half of your brain is reserved for the kind of thinking that produces creative newswriting. The right cerebral hemisphere—the right side—is the area of the brain that performs the creative work of your mind.

By playing a series of mind games with yourself—and particularly by adopting a style of outlining that is tailored to your brain's creative bent—you can more successfully tap that inherent creativity. First, however, let's lay the groundwork.

EXPERIMENTS HAVE SHOWN that the "right brain" thinks, for the most part, in ways that its owner cannot verbalize. The artistic, creative impulses you feel when ideas suddenly fall into place are produced by the right hemisphere. When it is time for your mind to put a collection of concepts, symbols or emotions into perspective—to glean some emotional truth from a bunch of jumbled elements—it is your right brain that goes to work.

The impulses that produce poetry and music originate on this side of the brain. So does intuition. So does the ability to perceive spatial relationships—the ballet dancer's uncanny ability to maneuver between two partners, leaping and twisting through a small opening without colliding with anyone.

The left cerebral hemisphere, meanwhile, is responsible for carrying out the better-known, "rational" functions of everyday life. It deals with step-by-step arrangement of words, numbers and intellectual tasks. It thinks in sequential patterns. The work of mastering speech and arithmetic and logic goes on here. The mental work of, say, a Marine drill sergeant—or anyone else who concentrates on going by the book—is primarily dependent on the left brain, too.

The right and left sides work together, and we are never conscious of the complex, sometimes mysterious "cross-talk" that goes on between the two halves. Yet it is the precision of this communication between the two sides that seems to determine how well a reporter handles thousands of maneuvers that call for him to quickly balance and alternate between his logical and emotional talents.

LET'S CONSIDER AN ISOLATED PROCESS, speech, which is usually the domain of the left cerebral hemisphere. Remember the leukemia story? You're trying to tell the editor that the boy's battle will be a good story because it illustrates both exceptional courage and agony. Your ability to appreciate that concept is developed in your right brain. But the right brain has only the simplest verbal skills; it cannot express that appreciation. So the impulse is fed to the left brain, whose neuronal structure is more directly hooked up to the human speech system. Out comes your explanation.

In interviewing or writing, the key is often the ability to merge a hard, cold instinct for facts with a sensitive manner. The most interesting writers seem to be better at merging the two sides of their brains than the rest of us. With no specialized training, they have developed the most precise methods of exploiting their right-brain talents. They know when to push themselves for a creative solution, and when to stop pushing—to wait and let their unconscious, subjective side do the work. They have a strong, inexplicable belief that the proper impulses and flashes will bubble to the top.

When they need inspiration, when they need that unique feature angle that just won't seem to come, they instinctively turn the job over to their creativity filter, which is housed in their right brain. The right brain won't put the story into words for them—it probably can't. Instead, it will explore the story in a deeper fashion. It will look for the parts and the wholes—the relationships between the facts and the story's essence.

Your left brain may be counting the trees; your right brain is concentrating on the forest, examining how the trees fit in. Your left brain may be thinking that the leukemia victim has lived two and a half years longer than the doctors had predicted; your right brain is asking questions like, "How does this event relate to contemporary medicine, the family's expectations, the boy's emotions?" Your left brain looks at how things are; your right brain wonders how else they might be. The right brain rummages through dozens of possible combinations of facts, always with an aesthetic sense, a desire to make things "fit."

Think about it. Do you know the feeling of being so engrossed in your work that time stands still? That everything around you—noises, voices, movement—is shut out? When you sense all the pieces of a story falling into place? When something inside of you says, "Hold on, that's *it!*"? In those moments, the right half of your brain has taken charge. You have stepped outside the narrow, left-brain way of looking at things—one piece of information after another—and are now working at a different level of consciousness, a state of mind in which you expose your information not merely to your rationality but to your intuition; not merely to your intellectual depth as a reporter but to your emotional depth as a human being. This must be done. You must develop the confidence to shift into this way of thinking so that you can sufficiently "play" with the facts you've gathered, shifting them around in your head, knowing that when you find the right combination, a spark will go off inside you.

THE RIGHT-BRAIN THEORY HAS BECOME exceptionally popular since the mid-1970s. In fields like education, business management and medicine, a wave of specialists, conferences and books on the subject have sprouted. Each begins by describing how the right brain works, and then insists that once you're aware of the left-right relationship, you can benefit from it.

The best example of how to teach yourself to consciously make use of the right-brain concept is contained in *Drawing on the Right Side of the Brain* by

Betty Edwards, an art instructor who began tailoring her instruction to right-brain ways of thinking more than a decade ago. She explains to her students how the left brain's sequential and verbal biases make it difficult for the average person to liberate his artistic impulses, and then tries to teach them how to "experience" the shift into a "Right-Mode stage of consciousness." She wants them to force themselves to stop thinking in words, and to concentrate on letting the visual image in their mind slide directly onto the blank sheet of paper, not allowing the left brain's verbal interpretation of the image to get in the way.

There is often a peculiar feeling when one tries to shut off the left brain (an act that's virtually impossible, scientifically speaking, but don't let that stop you; it's more important to imagine that a pure right-brain stream of thought is achievable). See if Edwards's anecdote sounds familiar:

> One artist told me, "When I'm really working well, it's like nothing else I've ever experienced. I feel at *one* with the work; the painter, the painting, it's *all one*. I feel excited, but calm—exhilarated, but in full control. It's not exactly happiness; it's more like bliss; I think it's what keeps me coming back and back to painting and drawing."

In art, the right-brain concept leads to techniques such as using "negative space," drawing with most attention paid to the white shapes that develop between the artwork and the edge of the paper as the drawing progresses. Again, the intent is to break the would-be artist away from his left brain's fixation with literally interpreting the object that is being drawn.

"The negative spaces, bounded by the format, require the same degree of attention and care that the positive forms require," Edwards says. "Beginning students generally lavish all their attention on the objects, persons or forms in their drawings, and then sort of 'fill in the background.'

"It may seem hard to believe at this moment," she tells her new students, "but if care and attention are lavished on the negative spaces, the forms will take care of themselves."

In newswriting, the right-brain concept fits snugly into the process all writers go through. They search their minds for an "angle"—an emotional impulse, a direction, a flash; often it's a feeling they can't put into words, but it gives them the first clue about how to tell a story. That's the right side at work.

From there, they begin finding words to fit into that concept (left brain). As the story develops, they look for other subangles; other twists (right brain); once they find them, they return to the process of phrasing (left brain).

Over and over, the unconscious shift: The right cerebral hemisphere produces the creative impulse that sends you in the proper direction; the left hemisphere performs the equally complex chore of putting the words and graphs into a precise sequence.

OKAY, THAT'S THEORY. Now, how do you make it come alive? How can you heighten it?

One of the best and easiest techniques is to adopt a style of outlining that forces your right brain to go to work, a style that tries to shut off the sequential side of your mind and liberate the other. This is an interim step. It should occur between the time you begin feeling a vague sequence develop and the time you prepare a standard, graph-by-graph, vertical outline of your story.

First, take an unlined piece of paper. (Lines might put your mind in a step-after-step, left-brain framework.) Draw a circle in the center of the page, and inside the circle write a word—a "slug"—that best defines the story's central theme.

Now, as soon as any related concept or issue or point or feeling in the story strikes you, write a one-word symbol for it somewhere else on the paper, draw a circle around that word, and draw a line connecting it to the main circle. Just wait for the feelings to arise, and then mark them down wherever they seem to fit—above, below or off to the side of the main circle.

Thus you're creating an outline that lets the components float in space, giving you a better chance to visualize the many relationships between them.

Diagram 9.1 is an example of what a simplified right-brain outline of the leukemia story might look like. If you study this kind of outline while you mull over a more formal sequence, it will become easier to find an angle that goes beyond the straight facts, so that you don't have to settle for dull, everyday approaches like:

> A five-year-old boy has won a three-year struggle with leukemia despite his doctors' predictions that he would live only six months.
> The parents of Darnell Thomas say they are . . .

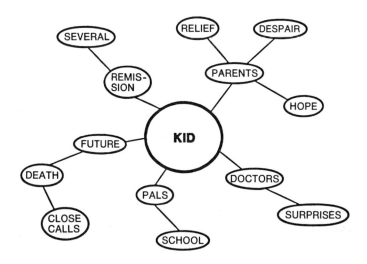

Diagram 9.1. *A simplified right-brain style of outline.*

Let's examine a right-brain outline of a far more complex story—a news analysis of a Philadelphia program that had dramatically cut the number of street gang deaths. The story was tricky not merely because it combined statistics, politics, bureaucracy and atmosphere, but because it was being written for a Los Angeles newspaper. It attempted to contrast Philadelphia's success with Los Angeles's failure in controlling street gang violence. Thus in composing it, the reporter had to quickly bounce a succession of variables off each other—a narrative that illustrated Philadelphia's problem, followed by a statistical summary of Philadelphia's success; then, quickly, to provide the article's perspective, a summary of Los Angeles's problem with controlling gangs, and Los

Angeles's voids; then back to a capsule description of how Philadelphia's program worked.

The reporter knew that unless he handled these elements with great coordination, the reader might need to read ten or fifteen paragraphs to gain the required base of knowledge. Like a motion picture director who senses his audience won't sit through fifteen diverse, unrelated "establishing" shots at the beginning of a film, the reporter had to put a premium on streamlining—something he could achieve only by organization. In Diagram 9.2, you can see the number of tentacles that flow from the reporter's central concept, "CRISIS."

Only after the reporter had allowed his story elements to "float" was he ready to work on a sequential outline. He first had to give his mind a chance to examine the periphery of the story as well as the center. He first had to look for the pieces that best exploited the essence of the story, the ones that would make the reader feel the way he felt. He needed to look for something—some conversation, some quote, some gesture—that defined the story in terms of the reader's life. Ironically, in this case the effort was unsuccessful. The reporter was unable to overcome the burden of presenting the statistical information, and the story appeared in a dry, factual style. But he knew he had pushed his creative faculties as hard as he could, and so he was satisified, even though he had failed to achieve his ultimate goal.

WITHIN THE RIGHT-BRAIN THEORY is an intriguing explanation of why some types of thoughts are so difficult to verbalize, and why some people

camouflage right-brain motives with left-brain rational-
izations. This concept is interesting because as a person
matures, he or she is usually confronted with an
increasing number of impulses that seem too complex

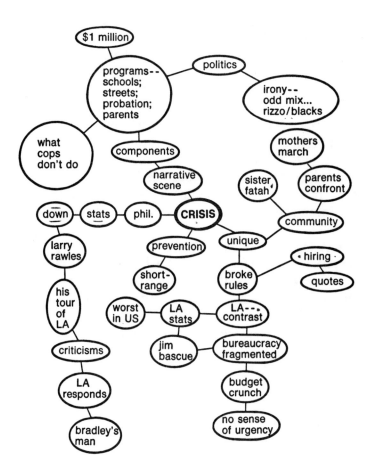

Diagram 9.2. A more complex story as seen by the right brain.

for words—and yet have to be acted upon. Personally and professionally, it's the same:

• An editor is shown a picture of a celebrity making an obscene gesture. He cringes and says, "OK, run it—but no bigger than two columns." Later, when his boss compliments him on his restraint, the editor may try to describe his rationale, but what he really did at the time was to subconsciously envision the tolerable level: how big the picture could be run to exploit its value without offending too many sensibilities.

At the moment he made the decision, he was acting on instinct. Two columns just "felt" right. Again, the right brain at work. Of course, editors and their bosses don't like to admit they run on such impulses—it sounds too chaotic, too unbusinesslike—so we usually hear other, more elaborate, left-brain explanations. Instinct? They don't promote you many places for your instinct.

• A husband and wife find a new apartment. All he emphasizes is the fact that it's smaller than their current apartment. The first thing that strikes her is its charm, the way the rooms are arranged, the angle of the cathedral ceilings. It just "feels" right.

The point: That "feel" has just as much intelligence behind it—was produced by the same electrochemical transmission in the brain—as the spoken reaction of the husband who says, "It's too small."

The husband and wife will have to argue the point, just as your own right and left hemispheres argue and then merge when the brain is called upon to process information.

Writers should understand this process not simply to

improve the management of their information, but also to help them deal with the often contradictory swirl of people they confront in their jobs. Can a successful young jockey really express why he is so much better than his competitors? Within himself, he may feel confident of his uncommon ability to sense a horse's instincts and to respond perfectly to those cues—but such perceptions are ordinarily controlled by the right brain. Can they truly be translated into a language that the left brain can express?

Or can a baseball player who hit a game-winning home run really answer the standard question, "What were you thinking about when you hit it?" Athletes suffer from a reputation for dumbness for giving stock answers to such questions, but it is not their fault that they cannot explain such things. Their skills are buried in a right-brain sense of physical unity, a feeling that usually defies verbalization. A hundred—a thousand—physical and emotional variables come together inside the batter at the moment the pitcher releases the ball. The right variables plus the right pitch equal a home run.

NO ONE EXPECTS TO SOON WITNESS a discussion among reporters in which one brags about an interviewing triumph that stemmed from "right-brain questions." We're talking about a concept that was born less than three decades ago; considerably more time is usually needed for laboratory work to filter down into the land of laymen.

It was in the 1950s that R.W. Sperry and Ronald E. Myers at the University of Chicago made the surprising discovery that when they cut the connection between the two halves of a cat's brain, each hemisphere functioned independently, as if it were a complete brain. Similar results were found in human patients when the researchers cut the nerve tissue that connects the right and left sides. (Such cuts were made in a successful attempt to prevent the spread of epilepsy from one part of the brain to another.)

Brain researchers had long known that the brain is a double organ, but evidence of the independent functioning of each half immediately produced a wave of new questions: Just how were the brains separate? Could they have separate thoughts, even separate emotions? How much did one hemisphere know about the other in a normal brain?

Today the answers are still being refined. The basic advantage of the dual-hemisphere system is simple: It allows us to separate the stimuli coming at us from the right and left sides. The nerve systems that operate the left side of your body are hooked up to the right side of your brain; the systems that operate the right side are hooked up to the left brain.

In recent years, some neurologists, troubled by the popularity of right-brain theories, have cautioned against oversimplifying the language of the brain. They are unhappy with the lack of formal proof that an individual can manipulate one side of his brain over another. Meanwhile, other researchers are presenting new possibilities.

For example, David Goodman, a Los Angeles psychobiologist studying the biological reasons for behavior, views the balance between the right and left hemispheres as only part of the picture. For him (the right-left separation of basic thought processes notwithstanding), the most important "two brains" are the forebrain—the frontal lobes—and the posterior section. It is the forebrain that appears to hold the key to powers of foresight, self-regulation, analysis and a "social sense"—an understanding of the needs and aspirations of others, he says.

As a person grows from child to adult, his forebrain develops and he begins to exhibit a sense of civilization. The now unpopular technique of frontal lobotomy demonstrated this. Patients whose frontal lobes were removed often began to demonstrate the traits of a twelve-year-old child, living only for the moment, concerned only with "me."

To truly exploit the brain's potential, one must integrate the talents of the right and left hemispheres with the forebrain, which provides for mature, far-sighted, disciplined use of mental talents, Goodman insists.

Others prefer a more simple and sweeping analysis of the right brain. Marshall McLuhan, the famed communications theorist, proclaimed that the right hemisphere has grown more potent than the left because of the glut of immediately available electronic information. The fact that so much data is simultaneously available to us appeals to the right brain rather than the left, he said, because the left half can take only one thing at a time—sequentially.

"For the first time in human history, electric information is underneath the right hemisphere and pushing it up, up, up," McLuhan said in 1978. "The old dominance of the left hemisphere depended upon lineality in organized road systems and production systems and so on. All the lineal-connected activities of man over the centuries supported the dominance of the left hemisphere, which is logical and, of course, legalistic."

His conclusion was a curt neurological explanation of the demise of culture: "If the left hemisphere is getting pushed down and the other one up, it means that music—rock 'n' roll and whatnot—is taking the place of literacy."

IN A WIDER SENSE, appreciating the respective roles of both halves of your brain has the potential to broaden your insight into the personality and talent of everyone you encounter.

Think about it. Suppose when you were a child in school, your teacher had talked to the class about the importance of feelings that cannot be expressed as words. Suppose you had somehow avoided the habit of assuming that you'd won an argument whenever your rival became tongue-tied. Suppose you'd never grown used to assuming: "Ah-ha! I've beaten him; he's at a loss for words; he's run out of valid thoughts."

Remember, there is a profound but mute intelligence at work in the right brain. The fact that an impulse does not cross over to the left half, where it can be routed to the speech center, does not dim its merit. Nevertheless, our culture employs its prejudice of taking no one seriously unless he can express himself in conventional speech (or establish himself as a genius in some other medium). A kid can't talk very intelligibly or intelligently, so he's rejected as "dumb." But wait—the same kid is a marvelous guitar player. He can hear you hum a complicated melody and duplicate it immediately on his instrument. Arrangement of words is a left-brain talent; the confluence of musical notes is a right-brain talent. Who's dumb?

This is not a plea to regard everyone as intelligent, or to believe that everyone has the potential to offer equally intelligent ideas. Certainly, you have had—and will continue to have—interviewing experiences or phone conversations with people who are wrong, stupid, inaccurate, unimportant, or all of the above. The key is to not tune them out immediately just because they *seem* that way.

The next time you encounter a person like that in your reporting, give him a chance in the context of right-brain talents. Give him the benefit of the doubt. Allow for the possibility that something important is being produced by his mind, and perhaps he simply can't get it out without help from the interviewer.

Think about the past. How much have you missed by not being more sensitive, by not recognizing that this person's thoughts could be as eloquent or as significant or as quotable as anyone else's, if only somebody— you—could make the effort to help him pull those thoughts out?

We can't predict such circumstances or solutions. But the next time you're faced with a situation in which a potentially good topic is being drowned by an inarticulate or uncommunicative subject, consider the possibility that he is holding back against his will. Try asking something absurdly obvious like, "Are you having trouble talking about this?" or "What do you find hardest to talk about?" Then ask why. Those questions may tap some hidden flow of words on some other channel, and who knows what you'll get?

Rest assured, you will waste time this way. But just

as certainly—although far less predictably—you'll find information or emotion that will improve your story, or possibly lead you to another one. That's what the game is about, isn't it?

Enough philosophizing. Let's get back to the newsroom.

10.

Creativity

ARE YOU GROWING TIRED of hearing our Ms. Turner praised to the skies? Well, hang on. Remember, she's our optimum, our goal—a personification of the kinds of skills we want to shoot for.

I'll level with you, though. The people who work with Turner get a little sick of her, too. She perplexes them. Why, they ask themselves over that second beer at the end of the day, is she the one who *unfailingly* comes up with the brilliant story idea or the unique angle? Why is she the one whose writing *always* seems to run in directions no one can anticipate? There is no predict-able "style" to her work, except that it seems to weave perception, logic and surprise in an endless stream.

Why, her colleagues groan, waiting for the third round to arrive, is she *different* from the rest? How does she do it? Can they ever know? She seems to revel in the mystique of her talent, to delight in somehow letting the story control her as much as she controls it.

We say such reporters are "creative," and we envy them, and we can't help being jealous—and yet we rarely stop to try to compare Ms. Turner's mental processes or output with our own, to see where our deficiencies may lie.

When we do, we find out that she has translated what are normally interpreted as personality traits into simple work habits. Magic? There is none. Her creativity is easily liberated because she has the discipline to take on challenging topics and the organizational skills to handle them. Her creativity filter reminds her not only to use strategies like right-brain outlining (as described in Chapter 9), but also to constantly *test* her free-flowing creative impulses with a long list of questions. To the degree she wishes to toy with a story—to take chances, to take risks—she must also firm up her methodology to make sure those creative impulses are pushed in the right direction.

THERE IS A LOT OF UNSEEN PAIN IN THIS. Turner rarely feels completely satisfied; there are always new plateaus for her creative energies to reach. That is one of her demons—the tension that builds when her subconscious begins to prod her. The moment, for example, when she recognizes a story that should be written, and knows that it will be a frustrating pursuit. It is the type of story no one else will go after; she could avoid it without worrying about the competition. She hates the idea of doing it, and yet she hates the idea of *not* doing it. She feels anxious, alone, worried by the possibility that she is venturing into lost territory; if no one else has yet written such a story, if no one else is interested now, perhaps it isn't a valid topic. Yet she also feels driven by a great sense of urgency. She is torn, knowing that ultimately she will be satisfied only by undertaking the story.

When she sits down to organize and write a complex piece, she is sensitive to each problem she faces. She can sense when her story elements provide an opportunity for creative handling—and, just as important, when to stop trying to toy with a story and bang it out straight.

She's a fluent thinker. She knows when she needs ideas, and can call up a great number of relevant ones from her memory, giving herself more combinations to play with—more potential story angles to choose from.

She's flexible. She can look at a style of story

structure that has solved dozens of tricky pieces for her in the past and realize that it won't get her out of this jam. She'll instead bend the old structure until it fits the new set of story components. If she stumbles upon a completely new pathway—a story structure she has never seen anyone try before—she does not cringe; she has the audacity to assume that she may be the one who will make a new style work.

She's a better analyzer than her colleagues. She understands the amount of gritty effort that she must put into studying her story components before the writing can begin. She understands that creative writing results from the new combination of old ideas, complex patterns formed from simple patterns, and the juxtaposition of elements that previously seemed unrelated. She has an unmatched talent for synthesizing, for redefining.

She concentrates on seeing through and beyond the obvious, the trivial. She prides herself on a deeper understanding of things. She considers herself able to penetrate further than her colleagues, to grab a topic and write the definitive version.

And sometimes, it all comes together. And sometimes . . . nothing works. But the effort is always there, the search for an opening, the attempt by the reporter to liberate her creative potential when the time is right.

HERE'S HOW SHE DOES IT—and how you should go about it. We saw in Chapter 9 that thinking in a right-brain frame of mind can unleash a writer's most intense artistic impulses. But to build a complete creativity filter, you need to give yourself more than a subjective edge; you must also study the way creativity is exhibited, and build a series of more objective tests that can be employed whenever you go looking for a creative solution.

To begin with, remember that our creative reporter is not as different as she seems. Her mind simply works harder at finding a pattern in the deluge of words, thoughts, events and readers that fill her life. She envisions the potential combinations of these forces, and picks the ones that best lead to story ideas and, subsequently, to story structure. She does all of this before she lays a finger on a typewriter, and what makes writing such an intriguing act is the knowledge that she will never do it perfectly. There are too many variables, too many unknowns for her to pull all the forces into harmony. If she can walk away from a project having achieved 90 percent of what she dreamed of, she feels wildly successful.

Sometimes, Ms. Turner's struggles sound like those of a woman on the verge of a psychopathic act, and if you're fond of Sigmund Freud, you may agree that there is little difference between the burden of a creative flow and an epileptic fit. Freud saw man unavoidably plagued by discontent as the result of conflict between his unconscious sexual and aggressive impulses and society's constraints. To reconcile the two pressures, he said, man seeks "defense mechanisms." If the mechanism is considered unacceptable by society—say, molesting eight-year-old girls—the man is labeled maladaptive or psychopathological.

But if the defense mechanism is one of sublimation—one in which he directs his energies into culturally approved behavior, such as writing or painting or boxing or political campaign organizing—society usually treats him well.

Creativity, Freud said, involves abandoning the world of reality for fantasy to provide an outlet for unsatisfied unconscious energies. Yet when you read any writer you admire, you can see that his injection of creativity is controlled. Had he indulged himself any more, had he not kept as much controlled balance between reality and fantasy, his approach to the story would not have worked. The closer you get to the edge, the more careful you need to be.

All great thought, all invention, rests on this balance, and yet the news business—like most other businesses—rarely takes it into account. News operations are structured on the same kind of flow-chart, chain-of-command, area-of-responsibility mentality that most large enterprises use. When editors are trained (normally an unplanned, helter-skelter process), it is with an eye to structure. They are becoming "managers." They have obligations to certain deadlines and processes. They have a loosely prescribed quota of stories that should be produced each day or week or month. They rarely are warned by their supervisors to give equal consideration to news-gathering proposals that don't quite fit into the paper's organizational structure.

THE MANAGEMENT OF CREATIVITY ("the scheduling of invention," one researcher wryly calls it) has drawn considerable study since World War II. Courses on the management of research and development now flourish, but it seems impossible for them to reconcile the unpredictable, illogical thread of creativity with the fact that managers must constantly focus their efforts on *controlling* the activities of other people. The nature of creativity is that it breaks from established patterns and rules. How can a boss tolerate that and still run his system?

That question does not have to be answered in the newsroom; it merely needs more consideration by editors and reporters. Early in this book, we offered Rule Number 1 ("There Are No Rules") as something to keep in mind when pondering mental attitudes. Rule Number 1 is also a helpful guide inside the newsroom. If an idea is good, who cares how many rules it breaks? Give it a chance, test it, weigh it, but don't dismiss it outright. The rule causes a lot of grief, but it also produces greatness.

Editors and reporters have to look more closely at how well creative powers are being used. Many news reporters develop only a fraction of their talents because they work for editors whose ability to articulate judgment doesn't go beyond descriptions like "bright," or "cute," or the ever-present "reads well." Not working under a literate, refined system of criticism, the reporter faces a long, painful struggle to learn his own flaws and correct them by comparing his stories with those of better, more experienced reporters. Certainly, if he has the desire he can improve in that fashion, but why make it so hard on him? Why not give him some help?

A sensitive editor can save a reporter literally years of heartaches by offering a single sentence that sums up a dilemma the reporter may feel but can't interpret. Imagine a young reporter whose feature stories are excessively flamboyant (too sugary, too eager, the product of strained writing) being told by an editor, "I'd like you to do a better job of combining your uninhibited, impulsive ideas with rational control. I mean, you can be silly, but when you get that way, it's more important than ever that you concentrate on disciplined silliness."

Not enough editors like to talk about balancing extremes. Most of them would shoot the kid down. What they and their reporters should be concentrating on is *when* to go searching for a creative impulse and what to expect. Here are some considerations. As you read them, think about the stories you've had trouble writing, or ones that you've read with disfavor.

DO THE RIGHT CONDITIONS EXIST?

• Do you have enough related material in your memory to produce a clever or inspired angle for this story? If you've interviewed a Jewish immigrant from the Soviet Union, do you know anything about that immigration controversy to augment the interview? If not, the possibility of a creative approach is limited; you're forced to rely on the elements that surfaced during your conversation, or to supplement your memory with research.

• How good a job can you do of sorting out the additional elements your memory feeds you? You may have triggered a heavy flow of peripheral ideas about immigration, or Russia, or Jews. Have you selected the proper ones to integrate into your story? Have you been influenced by the order in which they jumped into your head, or have you judged them on their merits?

• Did some of the story elements suddenly leap out at you? That can be a good sign, because one test of the creative thought process is the vibrancy of the elements that are to be combined—they must stand out from their surroundings.

• Do these impulses seem to be in a sufficiently free, unattached state? Make sure, because if the ideas you wish to combine are too rigidly tied to larger ideas, the new combination of thoughts you wish to construct may be artificial. You may wind up forcing an inappropriate or inaccurate structure. The right-brain style of outline is a valuable way of avoiding this hang-up, since it allows you to more clearly view the relationships among your facts.

Finally, if the conditions do seem to exist for a unique, creative combination of ideas, make sure that you have a feeling that the elements truly fit together, that they somehow merge like pieces of a jigsaw puzzle. If you can't feel that unity, you are probably kidding yourself.

ARE YOU BLOCKED?

How often has this happened? The spark has hit, you've decided that the story warrants a creative approach, you have finally executed a masterful idea on paper after extensive juggling—and now you're darned if you can figure out why it took you so long to go in the right direction. Why did you make so many wrong turns? Why didn't you reorganize the graphs sooner? Why did you have to spend two hours searching for the additional graph that brought the story into focus?

A variety of factors—most of them obvious, upon second thought—can block creativity. Be on the lookout for potential blocks and you'll have a better chance of avoiding them. Again, a good procedure when you do become stuck is to ask yourself some questions:

• Have you failed to correctly perceive and define the story elements? Have you fallen prey to wishful thinking and overrated the value of one or more elements? Were you overly ready to categorize your information? Did you judge it by its surface features, rather than by its significance? Did you forget the amount of energy that must be put into analyzing the story components and your goals for the story *before* you start to link various chunks of information into novel patterns? Experiments have found that the more creative scientific research worker devotes a proportionately larger part of his problem-solving activity to analysis; only after that analytical stage does he begin looking for a solution. Similarly, successful reporters often force themselves through an extra scan of their notes, resisting the temptation to rush to the keyboard and begin writing.

• Do you really have as much information as you need? Do you have too much, and are you possibly intimidated by the excess? Have you made use of the proper information?

• Has the syntax used by your sources cloaked your information in traditional terms and categories that prevent you from seeing the facts in a new, creative light?

• Is there something in your personal makeup that is keeping you from seeing essential story elements and their relationships? Are you carrying a prejudice, a desire to tell the story for a particular gain? Are you hamstrung by a drive to show off your background knowledge? Try backing off a bit; try composing with a slightly smaller degree of expertise; try being a little dumber in order to be a little smarter.

• Are you thinking the right way? You may be in the midst of *convergent* thought, in which a premium is placed on analysis and reasoning, but your story may defy that. The story elements alone may not lend themselves to a unique combination unless you bring something in from the outside. You may have to shift to *divergent* thinking, which emphasizes richness and novelty of ideas; it's a more playful way of solving a problem. Here's an example of a story that was written in standard, convergent style—and clearly could have benefited from divergent thinking:

> Despite President Carter's warning last week that all Iranians would be required to check with immigration officials before traveling overseas, international chess master Kamran Shirazi flew from Los Angeles to Munich Tuesday to visit his brother and inquire about European chess competition.
>
> The result: Immediately upon his return landing in New York, Shirazi was informed that he would be deported to Iran.
>
> "We thought everything would be OK," his young American bride of four months said tearfully . . . .

Now, look what could have happened if the reporter had been willing to shift gears and think in another direction. A small bit of divergent thought uncovers enough irony to grab the reader with far more force:

> In the game of chess, you can afford few mistakes.
> Kamran Shirazi, an international master at the game, made one too many.
> Despite President Carter's warning last week that all Iranians would be required to check with . . .

Only if the reporter was willing to turn to a concept not directly related to the step-by-step chronology of the news story could that angle be found. All stories require both convergent and divergent thought, but each story is solved with a unique blend of the two. You must modify your approach from story to story.

EACH OF THESE BLOCKS LEADS to the same essential question: Are you being stymied by forcing the wrong direction of attack? Are you being too rigid? Try to step away from the story. Remember, you need to balance a close involvement with the details of your story with a detached, imaginative view of the story's essence.

No matter how much you know about these blocks, sometimes that knowledge won't help. You'll suffer helplessly, waiting for inspiration, before giving up and cranking out an average piece. That's life. But don't be afraid to strain your mind the next time around. We have all been conditioned to fear our unconscious processes, to distrust them, to rely strictly on logical, rational forms of reasoning and writing; it takes courage to continue to give your intuitive side a chance.

If you're lucky, it will lead to a heightened feeling that will make up for the routine nature of the majority of news work. Just the chance to test your creative powers to their limits once or twice a month is an opportunity most people would pay dearly for, if they only knew the emotional rewards.

For centuries, artists have spoken with awe of such experiences. Beethoven would visualize and hear his instrumental music in its entirety while composing, and found there remained nothing for him to do but write it down. While composing *The Creation,* Haydn described a state of almost painful excitement: "My body would feel like ice, and then again, as if glowing in feverish heat." Others talk about words flowing spontaneously, against their will, so fast that the pen or typewriter could scarcely follow. The work became autonomous. The characters in a novel assumed an independent existence and took control, leading the writer where they wished. Sometimes these moments resembled a trance; other times, the artist or writer was led along by a strange rhythm. Some were propelled by that fear that unless an idea was worked on immediately, it would be lost.

And then, finally, the words would be on paper. A sensation of relief would begin to sweep over them— and then, just as suddenly, they would have to check and double-check their work, afraid that they were wrong, afraid they had been carried away by a magical force too powerful to be confined by logic.

"He to whom this emotion is a stranger," Albert Einstein said, "who can no longer wonder and stand rapt in awe, is as good as dead."

11.

Schizophrenia in Editing

THE LAST WORD HAS BEEN TYPED. It's over. You give yourself an invisible pat on the back and breathe a well-deserved sigh of relief. For four days you pushed that story, and now the pressure's off, and you ease up.

You just made a big mistake.

What you should be doing at this moment is pumping yourself up, becoming more vigilant, assuming a new perspective on the story, preparing to give yourself what doctors call a second opinion.

"That's the editor's job," you say.

Wrong. It's your job. It's the final mental filter in our chain: the ability to harshly edit your story through another pair of eyes before it leaves your desk. The skill of looking at your masterpiece with a less romantic, much colder feeling—an attitude that challenges the choices you made during the composition phase; an attitude that doesn't presume that those choices were the right ones merely because they were hard; an attitude that understands the imminence of print, and is even a little afraid of it.

This "self-editing" filter is another stage that too many reporters take for granted. Their failures cause a lot of little, hidden problems and unnecessary grief, and also painfully illustrate the void that lies between the points where a reporter's responsibility ends and an editor's begins.

The central fact is this: Most reporters in most news organizations do not have a great deal of confidence in the people who edit their copy. Reporters who work for a very large news operation may be lucky enough to have the guidance of an editor who specializes in the subject they're writing about, but usually the copy goes straight to the city desk, where it is read under pressure of time and volume, and then to the copydesk, where the editors usually concentrate on errors of commission, not omission.

Many copyeditors are talented, but you should not rely on them. As we have stressed throughout this book, to develop your professional skills to the highest degree, you must become more self-reliant. You must seek out the hard choices. You must be willing to try to fill the little leadership gaps that plague all news operations.

WHAT AM I ASKING YOU TO DO? I am asking you to become selectively schizophrenic. I'm asking you to develop the ability to shift gears after you finish typing and before you start editing.

At that moment, *become* an editor. Adopt the attitudes and perspectives that go with the job. Set your story aside for a minute, get up for a drink of water or walk around the office, and then return to your story with the eye of another person—somebody who has only peripheral familiarity with the subject of your story; somebody who will demand that the story snap out its essence, that its phrasing flow logically, that its purpose be clear.

That way, you are more likely to edit your story with the same level of intensity that helped you write it. The bursts of energy that came during the typing process may well have resulted in a variety of common oversights. We accept this, because the best reporters inject a power into their writing that overshadows appreciation of tiny detail. When you have a truly good story going, tiny detail is often not the first thing on your mind; you're grooving, the words are hitting, you're looking at the broad impact of your piece.

Which is why surprisingly obvious mistakes can creep into an important story, even though the reporter has broken his back to collect and present the information. A crucial piece of background information may be missing; a key figure in the story may be named without sufficient explanation of his importance; the perspective paragraph (Chapter 7) may not be there. In all those cases, the reporter had dealt with the material so many times while preparing the story that he gradually began taking some elements for granted; he subconsciously began assuming that they were common knowledge.

In Chapter 6, we talked about knowing the reader as a safeguard against those kinds of mistakes. But since no one's perfect, we have to build in a second line of defense: your ability to edit your copy.

Don't count on your editors to do this. How can they guarantee you that they'll always have the time—or the capability? Certainly you want them to review the story eventually, but for you there's a more important concern: to control your work to the greatest degree possible.

By nature, the average copyeditor likes to avoid problems. When a passage in a story bothers him, he first tries to simplify—deleting a troublesome sentence, or adding six words by hand. Because of the pressure he's under, or his lack of familiarity with the story, he is far less likely to *amplify*—to rewrite a paragraph, expanding it for precision. You're far better equipped to do that—if you can catch your own mistakes.

SO WIPE YOUR MIND CLEAR. Take a deep breath. Concentrate. Use your imagination. Become someone else. It's nothing more than a game you play with yourself. Turning back to the typed story with a pencil in your hand, you've become Mr. Hyde, determined to put the work of the reporter, Dr. Jekyll, to the test.

Let's see what Jekyll has done. Here it is, a two-thousand word analysis of a one-year-old local rent control law. You, Hyde, don't know a lot about the background of the story you're holding, and that's all the better. Jekyll spent four long days on it, and who knows how much he wound up taking for granted? You, Hyde, will take nothing for granted.

• *First paragraph.* Jekyll's story leads off with the fact that the area's landlords have had little luck in obtaining higher rents since the rent control law went into effect. But there's some important perspective missing here—the fact that the rent control law not only made rent increases hard to obtain, but also rolled back most rents to the previous year's level. Hyde finds this information when he gets to the sixth graph. Jekyll put it there because he was worried about its messing up the flow of his syntax; he talked himself into believing that the average reader knew of the rollback provision. Hyde is more objective. He weighs perspective against flow, decides that perspective is more urgent in a weighty analysis like this, and moves the rollback information up to the second graph.

• *Third paragraph.* A small overstatement that Jekyll hoped would give a more substantial tone to the story has caused a problem. He is writing about "a strong majority of landlords" surveyed by a poll, when in fact that majority was 56.2 percent. "Strong"? Hardly. Hyde kills the adjective.

● *Fifth paragraph.* Jekyll had this idea for a week and a half—a great image, he kept telling himself—and he was determined to use it. He wanted to describe the new power of the city's rent control board by saying, "The city's rent control establishment finds itself in the driver's seat. Local landlords, meanwhile, have their feet tied to the rear bumper of that driver's car, and are being dragged along cracked pavement."

Jekyll couldn't wait to put that in the story, but Hyde reads it with no such enthusiasm. In fact, Hyde realizes, there is more important factual material here— Jekyll has actually put together a good statistical analysis of a rent control system which had previously been described only by generalized rhetoric from landlords and tenants. With none of the ego problems that have hung up Jekyll, Hyde bumps the passage down into the eighteenth graph, and later in the day deletes it. Hardly a great image, Hyde notes ruefully.

AS WE'VE SAID, IT'S A GAME, but you have to play it. You have to invent ways to stay in control. If reporter-turned-Hyde doesn't get the story in shape, the werewolves of London on the copydesk—with a far less personal stake in the matter—will take over. And to the degree they sense the writer was not in control of the story, their willingness to make changes grows. Don't let them see any blood.

Some of this Jekyll-Hyde game playing is needed because deadlines make it impossible for you to let your story sit overnight and view it with a physically fresh eye the next day. But even when you have that luxury of time, concentrate on making this mental reporter-to-editor transition. Develop pride in your ability to subject your story to the most critical kind of dispassionate editing. Then think about parlaying that talent into better writing.

The relationship here, as with so many of the dynamics in newsthinking, is mathematical. To the extent you trust your editing ability, you can begin taking more risks as a writer. As Hyde's critical faculties are strengthened and sharpened, Jekyll's freedom to experiment is enhanced. For example, he can try beginning a story with four one-word paragraphs, no matter how dubious the technique seems, because he knows his editor alter ego will tear it up if it doesn't work.

Without Hyde, Jekyll might keep his creativity under wraps. Unless he was, say, 80 percent sure a style of writing or logic would be effective, he wouldn't attempt to use it. With a watchful Hyde, Jekyll can play with an idea at the typewriter even if he's only 10 percent sure it's a good one. Maybe—just maybe—by the time it is translated from his mind to the keyboard, it will work. Hyde will let him know.

Great reporters develop this confidence to take risks. There will always be times when Hyde's judgment will not suffice and you'll have to bounce an idea off a real editor; there will be other times when Hyde will simply be wrong, and your editors will tell you you've gone too far.

Schizophrenia in editing is this book's final filter, but it is probably the first thought strategy that will result in some immediate payoffs. By concentrating harder on editing your copy, you should quickly begin to catch flaws.

As for the majority of the other filters, especially ones like creativity and sequencing, we're appealing to a long-term goal, a hope that a year from now you can look back at your work and see an improvement, an awareness. There should be more sensitivity, more perspective, more variety, more intelligence. We're hoping this will have come about because you were willing to think about your talents in higher, more challenging terms; because you were willing to engage in some deep professional and personal introspection. That change doesn't happen overnight, and nobody can help you achieve it; it comes from your soul if you want it badly enough.

It's a long, hard climb. To make sure you get through it in one piece, read the next—and last—chapter.

12.

Coping with Pressure

STRESS IS OFTEN USED AS a synonym for pressure, but technically it is the *response* of the body to any demand made upon it. (Scientists refer to the cause of stress as the *stressor.*)

In the last forty years, Dr. Hans Selye of Montreal, the world's acknowledged leader in stress research, has dramatically expanded interest in stress by pinpointing the body's response technique, a mobilization of defensive reactions involving the pituitary and adrenal glands. This same reaction occurs in response not only to physical injury, but also to a wide range of psychological condi—

Wait! Who has time to *talk* about this? The phone on your desk in the newsroom is ringing! C'mon, pick it up. On the other end you hear an angry voice preparing to tear into you for the story that appeared in yesterday's paper.

Now, you broke your back on that story and you're already a little peeved about not receiving as much praise as you expected. As the caller's attack continues, your brain launches a process as old as your cave-dwelling ancestors. It prepares you to fight back. You can feel your insides tense as you prepare your verbal comeback.

There will be a crucial difference between you and the caveman, however. As the caveman saw his attacker coming, his endocrine system began producing the arousal hormone adrenaline, which alerted and aroused the body by mobilizing sugar into the blood and redistributing it to the body's potential "action centers." Later, as the conflict began, his nervous system released a larger amount of the chemical noradrenaline, which helped maintain blood pressure.

But in your telephone clash, there is no violence; there is merely the *anticipation* of it. As a result, your body releases mostly adrenaline, not noradrenaline. You are aroused, ready—needlessly. The visceral part of your brain has detected a physical threat, and has placed your body's defense mechanisms on alert, even though there is no physical danger.

AND THAT CAN CAUSE PROBLEMS. Dr. Selye and others have found that the rush of chemicals in these repeated, unneeded stress reactions has disturbing physical effects. It can cause physical illness, such as ulcers and hypertension, and an unpredictable array of mental problems as well.

That rush is what you're getting on the phone this minute. You put down the receiver, having argued back successfully, but still feeling a peculiar sensation that most of us write off as anger. Subtly, however, the damage has been done.

Pressure of even the most temporary variety can sap your mind's ability to process information, so you have to be on guard, regardless of how resilient you think you are. It is sadly inevitable: By the late twenties and thirties, bodies begin to feel the strain. What were once little pressures begin to take a heavier toll. Parents die, marriages break up, children are born and raised . . . you can run but you can't hide. Life's pressures *do* increase, and it becomes harder to keep up with any job—particularly a news job—without bending.

You may be in college—too worried about where to find a job to mull over the question of adjusting to one—but file the contents of this chapter in a corner of your mind just the same. It will come in handy. For now, let's get back to that angry caller in the newsroom and the angry response that began to well up inside you.

In any news operation, you're certain to find reporters and editors who, somehow, enjoy that sort of confrontation. They seem to seek it out. Sometimes, they appear to act like a drug addict looking for a fix, and in that light it is fascinating to consider a Canadian government study which said:

> Amphetamines . . . are in many ways similar to the body's own adrenaline. These drugs normally evoke an arousal or activating response not unlike one's normal reaction to emergency or stress.

Amphetamine addicts are called "speed freaks." They are often hostile, aggressive and suspicious. The news world is full of hard-charging reporters with similar behavior—and similar cravings. They have found a cheaper source of drugs: their own bodies. Yet they, like the speed freak, will eventually pay.

Various studies disagree on the amount of damage "occupational stress"—your workload, your pressures, your tendency to strive—does to your health. To many people, a sense of challenge and achievement in the face of some pressure is necessary for satisfaction. Yet news work is clearly an area where pressure can get out of hand, and where safeguards are too often lacking.

The body's misuse of the stress response, as described earlier, is only one example of how man's control of his environment has drastically outpaced his evolutionary progress. Consider your eyes. Only a thousand years ago, man used his eyes largely for long-distance tasks, like hunting and fishing. Now we spend much of our time doing close-up work, such as reading, and the resulting stress—the pressure on the eyes to adapt—has created a culture of myopes.

So it has gone with the adrenal gland's instinct for survival. The gland has yet to completely adjust to our rapidly acquired control of a once savage environment; it doesn't know the dinosaurs are extinct. It responds when it doesn't have to, and the result has been deadly to our culture of workaholics and strivers addicted to doing business at a compulsive, chaotic, aggressive, unhealthy pace.

OCCUPATIONAL STRESS STUDIES have grown increasingly popular, but there is little evidence of a researcher's having investigated the news business and the effects of its pressure (not even in Selye's 1,256-page landmark study, *Stress in Health and Disease*). Businessmen, skydivers, frogmen, air traffic controllers—even coastal fishermen and Israeli kibbutz members—have been studied, but we in news are left with less formal conclusions about the risks we take.

For example, there was the folksy little item the *Des Moines Register* printed recently, which quoted a small-town editor who quoted a farm bureau member who quoted a psychologist as saying, "The fear of drowning, bankruptcy or plunging into flames from an aircraft is less frightening than appearing like an idiot in print."

It is inevitable. No matter how much you enjoy pressure at work, you are continually confronted with the necessity of exceeding your tolerance. Gradually you adjust, and your tolerance level is raised a few more notches. And eventually you may reach a high, frightening cliff where you must choose between your health and your responsibility for doing your job the "right" way, as defined by yourself and your bosses.

No one can work in news without at least occasionally approaching that precipice. But you can control the frequency of such encounters by taking a hard look at your relationship to the job, by refusing to take for granted decades of prattle about the craft's unbearable pressure. You have to begin doing a better job of analyzing where your job pressures come from, and how often you needlessly encourage them. As Hans Selye suggests to his audiences: "You cannot control your mother-in-law, but you can control the way you respond to her."

It's not the pressures of work that screw up your mind and body—it's your *response* to the pressures. Begin by surveying the job and your response to its demands. Categorize the stress that you can control. Then start looking at the other kinds of situations— those in which you don't feel able to control your response to pressure. Here you have to look at the source of the pressure and try to limit it without losing your effectiveness.

DON'T FEEL GUILTY about admitting you're under too much pressure. In many offices, the credo is that you're not truly effective unless you're accomplishing your goals under strain, and for a while that works. You put a little more pressure on yourself, you push a little further, you absorb a little more tension, your work improves, you get more done. But eventually, you cross your line, an invisible barrier where pressure ceases to be beneficial and begins to erode your performance. Your body's reaction to pressure may first cause subtle changes in your physical stamina, making you increasingly vulnerable to mental errors as you work the same long hours. Where's the effectiveness in that?

The battle is to keep enjoyable, competitive hard work from being taken over by the insidious Protestant work ethic, a good idea that clearly got out of control. Four hundred years ago, French theologian John Calvin began insisting that every occupation—not merely the clergy—could be a "calling." You, the simplest of workmen, could assure yourself of a place with God by bringing to your work the qualities of thrift, honesty, abstinence and industry.

Today, newsrooms are littered with burned-out, barely alive forty-five-year-old reporters and editors, a bitter parody of the concept of work as religious pursuit. Thousands of men and women—victims of their own obsessive-compulsive behavior—have been sacrificed. Their jobs became cloaked in an unheavenly host of unhealthy—and often counterproductive—habits. The choice was between mere health and a career.

Because there hasn't been much of an effort in news work to fight that kind of momentum, you'll have to wage your own battle. If and when that vague feeling rears its head, suggesting that there is something wrong with the way you push yourself, take a while and look for a compromise—a balance, a level of physical and mental pressure that is good for you, a line you will try not to cross.

Gradually you will find that *you*—not just the news circumstances, not just your boss—are responsible for a certain percentage of line-crossings. The intensity you exhibit at work; the amount of time you spend rethinking a story you wrote the other day; the amount of anxiety you unleash worrying about career advancement—in all those cases, part of the pressure comes from a needless but persistent sense of obligation to be "serious," or to follow others' behavior. Don't fall for it.

Analyze your work environment and your perception of it, much as you scan the components of a story before you write. As in writing, there are important, sensitive choices to make. When is it helpful to push yourself, and when is it counterproductive? How have you built up unwarranted tension? How can you change your work routine without diminishing your effectiveness?

Unlike the process of newswriting, however, there is no "editor" here, no one ready to tell you whether you've made the right choice. You're on your own. Your decisions about how—and whether—to balance your pressure load won't be judged for years or decades, and even then only imprecisely, by your body.

As hard as they try to find ways to preserve the sanity of the "driven" businessman, psychological counselors keep coming back to the factor of motivation. If the executive believes that his compulsive behavior is vital to the organization, if he feels that a painful level of pressure is a price that has to be paid for success or respect, he cannot be pulled away from it. But once his perception is improved—once he realizes that many of his obsessive habits are *counterproductive* to his performance—he can force himself to change. He can work even harder without paying a physical price.

AWARENESS BUILDS THE ABILITY to control some of our response to pressure. That realization, in turn, builds confidence in our ability to reduce other stress factors, always with the goal of sacrificing only unneeded pressure, retaining the level of tension that works *for* us, pushes us in the right direction.

When job pressure plagues you, try making a rough mental list of the pressure points, the factors that seem the most stressful. A sample might include, in no order of importance:

Unpredictable overtime
Deadlines
Night work
Frequent fear of being unable to obtain vital information
Frequent letdowns when anticipated information does not surface
Fear of looking foolish in print
Distrust of editors, anxiety over lack of control once copy is in their hands
Anger, provoked by criticism
Prejudice, suspicion and hostility from uncooperative sources or readers
Lack of leadership or direction from editors
Inability to meet or understand editor's expectations
Continual demands to face the unknown
Constant awareness of what work is due "tomorrow"
Pressure for productivity at expense of quality

Boredom from insufficient assignments, lack of
    challenge
Need to play office politics in order to advance

How often does each situation surface? Is it more
likely to be caused by circumstances of the news flow or
by individuals? How often are *you* the individual
responsible for heightening the pressure? How often
does your performance improve as a result of your
willingness to put more pressure on yourself? How
often does your performance falter? When you put
more pressure on yourself, how often is it done with a
precise goal in mind? How often is it done out of a
general, obligatory feeling that you should be working
harder? Which of those two attitudes produces the best
results?

In short, separate the pressures that are uncontrollable and/or beneficial from the ones that are controllable
and/or unhelpful. Once you've made that distinction,
there are tougher decisions to be made: Of the
uncontrollable/beneficial   group—the   inevitable
pressures—which, if any, are taking too great a toll on
your emotions or your body? Is there room to change
the way you work? Is a more drastic change needed?

Advocates of "holistic" health, who claim that
physical and mental well-being are completely dependent upon each other, are trying to persuade people to
take a closer look at the connection between their work
and their bodies, between their professional and
emotional sides. They might tell you, for example, that
your personality helps determine whether you're better
suited for a morning or afternoon newspaper.

How? According to several studies made in the

1960s, the daily rise and fall of body temperature occurs earlier in the day in introverts; they are warmer and perform better than extroverts in the morning. Hence they figure to function better on an afternoon paper, where the key deadline work usually occurs before noon.

Other tests found that introverts tend to make better use of information stored in their memory (in-depth reporting) than extroverts, and that introverts make the best use of their powers if not driven hard (vulnerability to deadlines). Extroverts, on the other hand, tend to enjoy noise and bright colors, seem to actively seek stimulation and tend to remain stable under pressure.

The implications of such studies are obvious for an editor making story or beat assignments. For reporters, the evidence again underlines our theme: Are you working in the right kind of job? If the pressure load seems unbearable, is it possible you are having to fight too hard against your inadequacies?

THE EFFECTS OF PRESSURE usually first show up as fatigue, and it is here that our system of newsthinking filters can temporarily stave off the damage. Normally, fatigue saps your information-processing system in devious, often unfelt ways. There is little remedial action that can be taken when your long-term memory fails to supply a key connection with new information, or when your short-term memory isn't able to hold as many chunks of information as usual, or when your system of sequencing doesn't provide as many alternative combinations as usual, or when the story slides into print without a perspective paragraph. You're too tired to be aware of those voids.

At least, the average reporter is. Working by a casually constructed system, he isn't remotely aware of the order in which he usually processes a story, and so he doesn't know which steps are most susceptible to fatigue and which are the most important to preserve. He responds to pressure crudely—holding up as long as possible, but eventually caving in, accepting the inevitable slack-off in performance.

But with a conscious system of filters, you have a better chance of sacrificing as little as possible to unanticipated pressure and fatigue. When you feel things closing in around you, when you realize your mind is not working at normal capacity, start concentrating on the filters we've discussed in previous chapters. Make sure your story has been tested against each one. That checklist at least assures you that you've maintained your basic thought process.

Every skilled professional—doctor, pilot, athlete, you name it—has this kind of safety valve, a strategy to rely on when he or she gets into trouble.

As your sophistication allows you to combine several thinking or writing maneuvers into one step, you'll be able to operate with fewer conscious decisions than most reporters. Because your knowledge of story structure gives you a superior awareness of patterns, you'll have an edge in anticipating the kinds of decisions you'll have to make. Because you have polished your thought process, you'll need less effort to correct your errors. Because you understand the unity of listening, thinking and writing, you'll be better at pacing your work so that it remains within your capacity. You'll anticipate your weak spots; you'll head them off at the impasse.

This collective confidence will make you less anxious than the average reporter who shows up at work with a bad head cold, hoping to coast through the day, only to be confronted with an assignment to cover a detailed embezzlement trial.

Again, the solution is mathematical. When circumstances force you to cross your line of balance—to undergo more pressure than your maximum—measure how far across the line you've had to go, then increase your vigilance by the same amount. You can do this only if you have developed an understanding of your talents and limitations.

AND SUPPOSE, AFTER ALL THIS, you still can't keep things under control? Suppose you find yourself crossing your line of demarcation more frequently than you'd like? Suppose some deep need—the desire for constant success and approval, or for immediate gratification—just can't be met? Then you have to ask yourself The Big Question: Is it worth it? For too long, we have begun such introspection by asking an unrealistic question: "Am I cut out for news work?" Look. *Nobody* is cut out for news work, not the way it's practiced. It violates too many concepts of civilization. It asks you to throw out too much of your passion for life. It pressures you to trade spontaneity for logic. It commands you to quantify a world that resists cut-and-dried descriptions. And yet, somehow, it has a magic about it, addictive enough to pull you along. When you are no longer sure it is worth it, ask yourself the real questions: "Are the sacrifices I have to make in my personality in order to work in news worth the effort? Am I willing to operate without ever reaching a consistent emotional balance? If that balance is my highest aspiration, where do further sacrifices have to be made—in my work, or in my personality?"

At conferences throughout the world, Hans Selye is constantly asked for his advice on how to cope with stress, and he persistently insists there is no miracle.

"The final solution is a psychological one," he says. "You must get people to adopt a code of behavior, a code that transcends politics."

A code that encourages the optimum blend of stimulation, arousal and conflict. A code that ties your feelings and your goals together, creating a level of tension that your body and mind will instinctively seek, much as you seek the proper volume when you turn your stereo on. Some people like it louder than others.

No one defines that level for you; the best they do is leave you to wallow in generalities like "uptight" or "mellow" or "together"—sluggish words, each with enough unpleasant connotations to drive any intelligent person away. In our business, there is precious little time or encouragement for you to pursue the search for the right level of pressure to govern your life. Yet unless you can construct such a state of grace, you will not fulfill your potential as a writer.

Bibliography

Writers who are interested in gaining a deeper scientific understanding of their mental prowess are advised to read Marilyn Ferguson's *The Brain Revolution* (New York: Taplinger, 1973) and Nigel Calder's *The Mind of Man* (London: British Broadcasting Co., 1970). Both books are written with an enthusiastic desire to guide the layman through a complex, hidden world.

For a superb illustration of how modern scientific principles can be used to build better work habits, read Betty Edwards's *Drawing on the Right Side of the Brain* (Los Angeles: J.P. Tarcher, 1979). While the book is written for artists, its spirit should inspire many writers.

Those inspired by the majesty of human skill and its evolution will find Jacob Bronowski's *The Ascent of Man* (Boston: Little, Brown, 1973) something of a bible, a wonderful philosophic foundation. The scientific exploration of these skills is covered in a far more technical but understandable examination by A.T. Welford, *Skilled Performance: Perceptual and Motor Skills* (Glenview, Ill.: Scott, Foresman, 1976).

Other resources used to develop this book include:

Bandler, Richard, and Grindler, John. *The Structure of Magic I*. Palo Alto, Calif.: Science & Behavior Books, 1975.

Bryan and Harter. "Studies in Telegraphic Language" and "Studies in the Physiology and Psychology of the Telegraphic Language." *Psychological Review*, Vol. 4 and 6 (1897).

Buzan, Tony. *Use Both Sides of Your Brain*. New York: E.P. Dutton, 1976.

Cooper, Cary, and Payne, Roy. *Stress at Work*. New York: John Wiley & Sons, 1978.

Dimond, Stewart. *The Double Brain*. Edinburgh: Churchill Livingstone, 1972.

Gazzaniga, Michael S. "The Split Brain in Man." *Scientific American*, August 1967.

Geschwind, Norma. "Language and the Brain." *Scientific American*, April 1972.

Halacy, Daniel S. *Man and Memory*. New York: Harper & Row, 1970.

Harper, Robert J. *The Cognitive Process: Readings*. Englewood Cliffs, N.J.: Prentice-Hall, 1964.

John, E. Roy. "How the Brain Works—A New Theory." *Psychology Today*, May 1976.

Jones, D. Stanley. *Kibernetics of Mind and Brain*. Springfield, Ill.: Charles C. Thomas, 1970.

Klatzky, Roberta. *Human Memory: Structure and Processes*. San Francisco: W.H. Freeman & Co., 1975.

Levine, Seymour. "Stress and Behavior." *Scientific American*, January 1971.

Luria, A.R. *The Working Brain*. New York: Basic Books, 1973.

McGuigan, F.J., and Schoonover, R.A. *The Psychophysiology of Thinking*. New York: Academic Press, 1973.

McLean, Alan A. *Occupational Stress.* Springfield, Ill.: Charles C. Thomas, 1974.

Michener, James A. *Sports in America.* New York: Random House, 1976.

Pribham, Karl E. "The Neurophysiology of Remembering." *Scientific American,* January 1969.

Rosner, Stanley, and Abt, Lawrence. *The Creative Experience.* New York: Grossman Publishers, 1970.

Russell, Bertrand. *The ABC of Relativity.* London: George Allen & Unwin, 1925.

Schlesinger, Benno. *Higher Cerebral Functions and Their Clinical Disorders.* New York: Grune & Stratton, 1962.

Selye, Hans. *Stress in Health and Disease.* Boston: Butterworths, 1976.

Suojanen, Waino W. "Addiction and the Minds of Man." Third Annual Southeast Drug Education Conference, May 1977.

————. "Creativity, Management and the Minds of Man." *Human Resource Management,* Spring 1973.

Triesman, Anne. "The Effect of Irrelevant Material on the Efficiency of Selective Listening." *American Journal of Psychology,* December 1964.

Welford, A.T., and Houssiadas, L. *Contemporary Problems in Perception.* London: Taylor & Francis, 1970.

Wilson, Edward O. "Animal Communication." *Scientific American,* 1976.

Index

Other Writer's Digest Books

Market Books
Artist's Market, 474 pp. $11.95
Craftworker's Market, 570 pp. $12.95
Fiction Writer's Market, 504 pp. $15.95
Photographer's Market, 549 pp. $12.95
Songwriter's Market, 400 pp. $11.95
Writer's Market, 917 pp. $15.95

General Writing Books
Beginning Writer's Answer Book, 264 pp. $9.95
Law and the Writer, 240 pp. $9.95
Make Every Word Count, 256 pp. (cloth) $10.95; (paper) $6.95
Treasury of Tips for Writers, (paper), 174 pp. $6.95
Writer's Resource Guide, 488 pp. $12.95

Magazine/News Writing
Complete Guide to Marketing Magazine Articles, 248 pp. $9.95
Craft of Interviewing, 244 pp. $9.95
Magazine Writing: The Inside Angle, 256 pp. $10.95
Magazine Writing Today, 220 pp. $9.95
Newsthinking: The Secret of Great Newswriting, 204 pp. $11.95
1001 Article Ideas, 270 pp. $10.95
Stalking the Feature Story, 310 pp. $9.95
Writing and Selling Non-Fiction, 317 pp. $10.95

Fiction Writing
Creating Short Fiction, 228 pp. $11.95
Handbook of Short Story Writing, (paper), 238 pp. $6.95
How to Write Best-Selling Fiction, 300 pp. $13.95
How to Write Short Stories that Sell, 212 pp. $9.95
One Way to Write Your Novel, 138 pp. $8.95
Secrets of Successful Fiction, 119 pp. $8.95
Writing the Novel: From Plot to Print, 197 pp. $10.95

Category Writing Books
Cartoonist's and Gag Writer's Handbook, (paper), 157 pp. $9.95
Children's Picture Book: How to Write It, How to Sell It, 224 pp. $16.95
Confession Writer's Handbook, 173 pp. $9.95
Guide to Greeting Card Writing, 256 pp. $10.95
Guide to Writing History, 258 pp. $9.95
How to Write and Sell Your Personal Experiences, 226 pp. $10.95
Mystery Writer's Handbook, 273 pp. $9.95
The Poet and the Poem, 399 pp. $11.95

Poet's Handbook, 224 pp. $10.95
Sell Copy, 205 pp. $11.95
Successful Outdoor Writing, 244 pp. $11.95
Travel Writer's Handbook, 274 pp. $11.95
TV Scriptwriter's Handbook, 322 pp. $11.95
Writing and Selling Science Fiction, 191 pp. $8.95
Writing for Children & Teenagers, 269 pp. $9.95
Writing for Regional Publications, 203 pp. $11.95

The Writing Business
Complete Handbook for Freelance Writers, 400 pp. $14.95
How to Be a Successful Housewife/Writer, 254 pp. $10.95
How You Can Make $20,000 a Year Writing: No Matter Where You Live, 270 pp. (cloth) $10.95; (paper) $6.95
Jobs For Writers, 281 pp. $11.95
Profitable Part-time/Full-time Freelancing, 195 pp. $10.95
Writer's Digest Diary, 144 pp. $12.95

To order directly from the publisher, include $1.25 postage and handling for 1 book and 50¢ for each additional book. Allow 30 days for delivery.

For a current catalog of books for writers or information on *Writer's Digest* magazine, *Writer's Yearbook*, Writer's Digest School correspondence courses or manuscript criticism, write to:
Writer's Digest Books, Department B
9933 Alliance Road, Cincinnati OH 45242

Prices subject to change without notice.